Grow Your Own Happiness

How to Harness the Science of Wellbeing for Life

Dedicated to Ivan Dharma,
With love always

Grow Your Own Happiness

How to Harness the Science of Wellbeing for Life

DEBORAH SMITH

aster

An Hachette UK Company
www.hachette.co.uk

First published in Great Britain in 2019 by Aster, an imprint of
Octopus Publishing Group Ltd
Carmelite House
50 Victoria Embankment
London EC4Y 0DZ
www.octopusbooks.co.uk
www.octopusbooksusa.com

Distributed in the US by
Hachette Book Group
1290 Avenue of the Americas
4th and 5th Floors
New York, NY 10104

Distributed in Canada by
Canadian Manda Group
664 Annette St.
Toronto, Ontario, Canada M6S 2C8

ISBN 978-1-78325-307-4

A CIP catalogue record for this book is available
from the British Library.

Printed and bound in China

10 9 8 7 6 5 4 3 2 1

Publishing Director   Stephanie Jackson
Art Director   Yasia Williams
Senior Editor   Alex Stetter
Designer   Sally Bond
Illustrator   Stella Chili
Production Manager   Caroline Alberti

Contents

How to Use
This Book

I wrote this book to share practical advice on how to grow your own happiness. It is full of tips and techniques to help increase your wellbeing and life satisfaction, and the many factors that can contribute to improve them, such as gratitude, positivity and resilience.

Each chapter contains an overview of one of the factors to give you an understanding of why it is important, and how it can promote your wellbeing and potentially act as a preventative measure against mental ill-health.

I discuss some scientific research showing the effectiveness of Positive Psychology and why I believe each factor in the book is important. Naturally, there is plenty more to say, but this book will provide more than enough information for you to start to grow your own happiness. The intention is for you to be taken on a journey of discovery, from start to finish, with each chapter building on the last.

Most of the exercises in the book are designed to be repeated. They are fantastic skills that can be learned and developed over time to help change your mindset into one that is beneficial to your wellbeing. They may eventually become part of your way of being and will require little or no effort. I have been running workshops using these techniques for many years and I love seeing people benefit from them, especially if they were unsure or dismissive to start with.

Each chapter can be read on its own and you will undoubtedly benefit from them as separate entities. But there is more benefit in understanding how the different factors affect each other and how they are all interdependent. As you develop one factor, you will also feel benefits in other factors. For example, the more you develop gratitude, the more you will notice your relationships improve. The more you develop positivity, the more you will notice your levels of resilience increase.

I recommend starting at the beginning of the book, focusing on one chapter at a time and spending a while developing each skill before you introduce another. Be careful not to adopt too many new behaviours at once or too quickly, as you may feel overloaded and will be more likely to give up. Ideally, take your time. Imagine the process as layers of concrete – you need to wait for one layer to set before you can add the next layer. Let your new way of being become strong before you add more. You want them all to take hold and support each other.

Throughout the book, there are a number of "Watch Outs". Think of these as a heads-up on potential pitfalls, common misunderstandings or dead ends that people often go down.

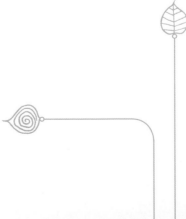

There are many themes running through this book, some of which
I repeat in different places. This repetition is evidence of their importance.
The most common themes are:

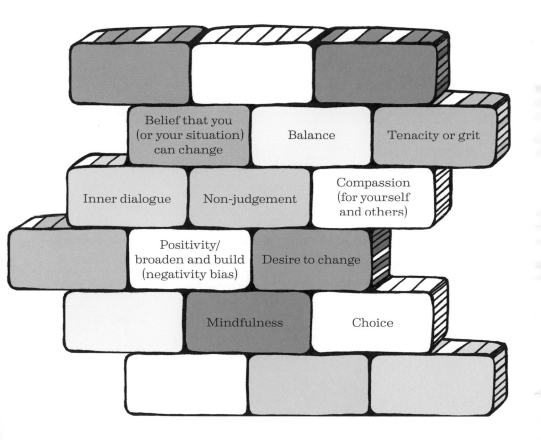

Don't worry if, at first, you don't completely get the themes and threads that reoccur. It is natural to understand them on one level now, and for it to suddenly click, giving you a lightbulb moment when you come to them again later in the book. Once you have finished the book and reflected on it as a whole, you might find moments where all the different threads and interconnected parts link up in your mind – at this point it's worth coming back and rereading the relevant chapters as they may make sense on an even more profound level.

I hope you feel this book is worthy of a reread, and you refer back to it over time. Never underestimate the power of planting a seed. As Einstein said: "I must be willing to give up what I am in order to become what I will be." I would add to the end of that sentence "...and *want* to be."

As your happiness grows it will bear more and more fruit.

Introduction

This chapter is an introduction to Positive Psychology, also known as the "Science of Happiness", the scientific study of wellbeing and happiness. One of the founders of the Positive Psychology movement, Martin Seligman, has defined Positive Psychology as "understanding and facilitating happiness and subjective wellbeing". Subjective wellbeing is how we view and feel about our own lives.

Positive Psychology also looks at the different factors that help us get through life as individuals or as a group, improving our happiness and wellbeing. And it's these beneficial factors that we will explore in this book – from gratitude to mindfulness – and show how you can use simple exercises and techniques to introduce them into your life with great results.

Remember, different factors will appeal to different people and it's best to find out for yourself which ones work best for you; *there is no right or wrong*. In fact, people often find that, as they change, so do the exercises that appeal to them most.

Allow yourself to be guided by what you like and enjoy doing most and don't try to force anything. Much like planting a seed, if the conditions are right, the seed will germinate and grow.

What is Happiness?

Happiness can be defined as "a state of wellbeing or contentment, a pleasurable or satisfying experience". To keep things simple, I will use the word "happiness" throughout the book, but it could be replaced by many other words, such as "wellbeing", "life satisfaction", "contentment", "harmony", "joy" or "fulfilment". Use whatever word is right for you. Words mean different things to different people, and it is not the specific word that is important but the essence of what is behind it.

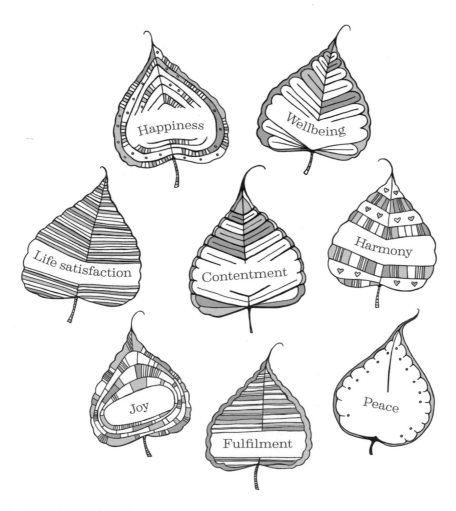

HEDONIC VS EUDAIMONIC HAPPINESS

The ancient Greek philosophers Aristippus and Aristotle believed that there were two types of happiness: *hedonic* and *eudaimonic*.

Broadly speaking, hedonic happiness is about getting as much pleasure as possible while avoiding negative emotions where you can. It is usually associated with short-term thinking, for example, getting drunk and having a good night out, without thinking about the long-term consequences.

Eudaimonic happiness leads to contentment through doing something with purpose and meaning. This type of happiness is associated with thinking in the long term – for example, the sense of life satisfaction that comes with getting closer to your life goals.

To make sure they both have a positive effect on you, and those around you, try thinking in the long term for both hedonic and eudaimonic happiness. In other words, enjoy yourself but be mindful of the long-term consequences of your actions. For example, enjoy buying a new piece of clothing but accept that the buzz won't necessarily last.

Eudaimonic happiness helps you keep your overall sense of life satisfaction and wellbeing at a good level and one that remains fairly stable despite life's inevitable ups and downs. Hedonic happiness has peaks and troughs according to your personal circumstances. Ideally, you will achieve a healthy balance between the two types of happiness – hedonic and eudaimonic.

What Determines Happiness?

Through extensive research, Positive Psychologist Sonja Lyubomirsky has concluded that our happiness is determined by three different factors: our genes, our circumstances and our intentional activity (what we think, do and say).

GENETIC FACTORS

Sonja Lyubomirsky believes that 50 per cent of our happiness is determined by our genes; in other words, we are born a pessimist or an optimist – it is set. This 50 per cent is not something we can necessarily change (our ability to affect our genes is discussed on page 211), but the remainder we certainly can.

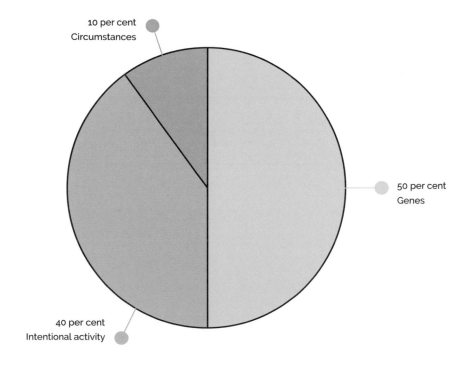

10 per cent
Circumstances

50 per cent
Genes

40 per cent
Intentional activity

OUR CIRCUMSTANCES

Our circumstances in life, for example, the conditions into which we are born, where we live and so on, determine 10 per cent of our happiness. However, this is the part that most people overestimate – we can spend a lot of our lives believing if we get a new car, a new place to live and more money, then we would be happier. The research tells us differently. This is why when people win the lottery, their happiness level often ends up the same as it was before they won (and sadly, some people even end up with their happiness lower than it was before).

Similarly, if people suffer a life-changing accident or ill-health then their happiness can return to the same level as before. Wherever your happiness level is before an event, whether "good" or "bad", it usually returns to that point, although the amount of time it takes to return to the same level does vary.

People can vastly overestimate the impact of big events, whether good or bad. Of course, it is possible to achieve greater happiness and life satisfaction after a major event, and the ability to go beyond your original base level is discussed in the Resilience chapter (see page 102).

Things vs Experience

Winning the lottery is an example of a life-changing event – and it is common to believe that suddenly becoming rich will make us happy. But we adapt to new circumstances more quickly than we think, and return to the same level of happiness or life satisfaction as before we had our big win. This is known as "hedonic adaptation".

I am not suggesting you never buy another dress or car, or whatever it is that you enjoy, but do recognize that the sense of happiness and joy will be relatively short lived. It's important to see this so you can avoid getting stuck on the "hedonic treadmill", where you are constantly shifting your focus to the next thing. For example, thinking about what you are going to buy next as soon as the feeling has worn off from your last big purchase.

Many people fall into this trap and it's easy to see why – we are surrounded by advertising for the latest phones, trainers and so on. This means it's easy to buy too much stuff we don't actually need. This is known as "stuffocation" and leads to cupboards full of toys that are hardly played with, and clothes and shoes that are barely worn. It's bad for our happiness as well as for the planet – overconsumption has a huge environmental impact both in the production and disposal of the goods.

However, James Wallman, the creator of the term "stuffocation", believes social media has helped to move our focus from material things to our experiences. Before social media, the things we bought were more visible – for example, people would wear their new watch for all to see. But now social media allows us to post photos of our holidays or evenings out and this means experiences are now perceived as more valuable than ever.

This shift could be a good thing because more life satisfaction is gained from experiences than from material things. However, there is a greater risk of making comparisons, which can lead to people feeling unhappy with what they are doing with their own life. This is how fear of missing out (FOMO) arises. Happily, this can be overcome through the practice of gratitude (see page 38).

INTENTIONAL ACTIVITY

Sonja Lyubomirsky believes that the final 40 per cent of our happiness is determined by what we think, do and say. And the good news is, we can have complete control over this amount. While we cannot affect our genetic makeup, and may or may not be able to affect our circumstances, we can definitely affect how we think and behave, thereby increasing our happiness and wellbeing.

> *This is the focus of this book – how we can affect our thinking and behaviour to increase our life satisfaction by up to a massive 40 per cent.*

These are not temporary fixes – you can permanently grow your own happiness if you choose to practise the exercises in this book. It's all about being empowered to take control, to learn and develop the skills you need to take charge of your own wellbeing.

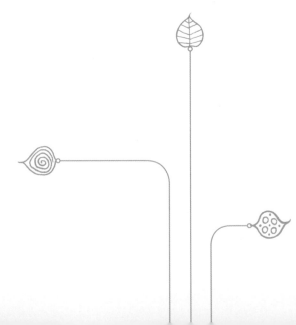

Try It Out:
How to Gain Maximum Happiness

You can increase your enjoyment of any experience by doing the three following things:

1. When planning an experience – for example, a holiday – imagine actually going there, so you start to enjoy the experience before you have even left the room. Our power of visualization is so strong that our brains don't distinguish between what we visualize and what we actually do. This is why sportspeople often use visualization to help them achieve their goals.

2. Be present while the experience is actually taking place. Don't fall into the trap of letting your mind drift. Be conscious of whether you are in the moment or whether you are thinking about work or an argument you had with your partner. You could be missing the fact that you're in peaceful, beautiful surroundings. We will look at this more in the Mindfulness chapter (see page 58).

3. After the event you can enjoy it all over again each time you look at photos, tell stories about what happened and reminisce – even years later, talking and thinking about it can bring back all the happy feelings.

Why Be Happy?

"Why care about happiness?" might seem like a silly question and, in some ways, it is because happiness is one of the things we all want. Not many things are universal, but the human desire to be happy is one of them.

However, when something is so common, it often becomes overlooked. We almost dismiss it as "Yes of course I want to be happy, doesn't everyone?" Then we strive for things that we *believe* will make us happy and put all our focus and energy into those things. The wonder of Positive Psychology is that it studies what can *actually* make us happy and how we can develop and maintain it.

So far, Positive Psychology has not come up with the answers we were expecting – we now know money and possessions do not bring happiness, nor does your state of health or where you live. In other words, your state of wellbeing can be good or bad, irrespective of these things. What we now understand is that happiness is not just a nice thing to have and something that we all want; we know that happiness has a further-reaching effect than we could ever have imagined. See page 33 for some of the benefits of happiness.

Are You at the Starting Line?

Are you able to cover your basic needs, such as food, clothes and a roof over your head, for yourself and any dependants you may have? I am not saying that you need these things in order to develop your happiness, but it can be more of a struggle if you are under a significant level of stress.

I am speaking from experience – 30 years ago, I was pregnant and homeless (see page 34). I assure you that you can get yourself out of any situation you may find yourself in if you choose to do so. But it is vital to believe that you can change and have the determination, tenacity and resilience to keep going even when things are really tough.

Before you read any further, it will help to establish whether Positive Psychology and the exercises in this book will be helpful to you right now or whether you might need the help of a regular psychologist or therapist to improve your wellbeing and get you closer to the "starting line".

The Positive Psychology exercises in this book will be helpful in whatever situation you might find yourself but, in my experience of working with people, if you are in deep depression for example, you might find it difficult to engage with the exercises. If this is the case, then contact your doctor or find a therapist who can help you improve your mental health using regular psychology techniques. In time, you will be ready and at the starting line to try the happiness techniques in this book.

Positive Psychologists vs Regular Psychologists

Positive Psychologists focus on happiness, wellbeing and functioning at your best, whereas regular psychologists can help better when something goes wrong on a psychological level, such as depression, anxiety or relationship problems. In short, both use techniques developed from the scientific study of the human mind, how it functions and why we behave in the ways we do, but they focus on different ends of the same scale.

The Mental Health Scale

To find out where you are right now in terms of happiness, try the Happiness Questionnaire (right). This will give you an indication of where you are on the scale of mental health.

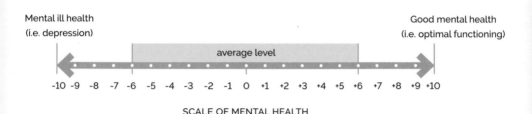

Mental ill health
(i.e. depression)

average level

Good mental health
(i.e. optimal functioning)

-10 -9 -8 -7 -6 -5 -4 -3 -2 -1 0 +1 +2 +3 +4 +5 +6 +7 +8 +9 +10

SCALE OF MENTAL HEALTH

Most people are somewhere between –6 and +6, that is neither depressed nor functioning at their best. If you fall within this range, Positive Psychology could definitely help you improve your wellbeing.

If it's –7 or below, talk to your doctor or find a psychotherapist or counsellor to help. If it's +7 or more, try the exercises in the book to get you even further up the scale and share your happiness with others – as discussed in the Relationships chapter (see page 178). Happiness is contagious so please pass it on!

Apr. 1st (first time) = 69

Happiness Questionnaire

Below are some statements about happiness. Note down how much you agree or disagree with each one, according to the scale on the left.

SCORE:

1 – *strongly disagree*
2 – *moderately disagree*
3 – *slightly disagree*
4 – *slightly agree*
5 – *moderately agree*
6 – *strongly agree*

THE STATEMENTS:

A I like who I am *4*
B Life is rewarding most of the time *5*
C I wake up feeling rested *5*
D I am optimistic about the future *4*
E I think the world is a good place *3*
F I have a group of good friends *5*
G I enjoy my job *4*
H I am happy *3/4*
I I have a positive effect on others *4*
J My life is not too busy and I have time for myself *4*
K I feel I am in control of my life *5*
L I often enjoy life *3/4*
M I have a sense of meaning and purpose in my life *4*
N I have fun with other people *4/5*
O I take care of my wellbeing *6*
P I have happy memories of the past *6*

Now add up all the scores to give yourself an overall measure of happiness.

Interpreting Your Score on the Happiness Questionnaire

Whatever your score, the good news is there are lots of skills you can use to increase your happiness level.

Between 16 and 32
This is the equivalent of –10 to –7 on the mental health scale on page 24.

This is a very low level of happiness. Are you aware of what's causing your unhappiness? Are you getting help for how you are feeling? Start by seeking professional help and reaching out to ask for support from family and friends.

Between 33 and 48
This is the equivalent of –6 to –3 on the mental health scale on page 24.

This is a low level of happiness, indicating that life may be tough for you right now and you are struggling to find things to feel happy or positive about. The exercises in this book will help – perhaps there's someone you could do the exercises with? It might help to find someone to support you and share your happiness journey.

Between 49 and 64
This is the equivalent of –2 to +2 on the mental health scale on page 24.

This is an average level of happiness, indicating moderate happiness and someone who is fairly satisfied with life. It is time to embrace the exercises within the book and propel yourself onto the positive side of the scale to increase your happiness. Try to surround yourself with supportive, encouraging people and enjoy the journey together.

Between 65 and 80 Apr. 15

This is the equivalent of +3 to +6 on the mental health scale on page 24.

This is a good level of happiness. You are happy with life and probably able to hold on to a certain level of happiness even when life is difficult. You are likely to be open and ready to take on the happiness exercises to let yourself really flourish.

Between 81 and 96

This is the equivalent of +7 to +10 on the mental health scale on page 24.

This is an excellent level of happiness. There are lots of benefits to being this happy, not only for yourself but also for those around you. Your life satisfaction, creativity, health and relationships will all benefit. Practise the exercises in this book to cement your wellbeing, so it remains high despite what life may throw at you. You might even want to set up a happiness group to share your happiness and help others achieve the same level of wellbeing – helping others further increases our own happiness too.

Getting Ready to Begin

It's best to be honest with yourself to help remove any barriers to success that you may have. Answering the following questions will help you start to recognize some of your barriers:

• What would it mean if you were happy – what might you gain and what might you lose?

• What is the advantage of staying how you are?

• Do you struggle with self-esteem, lack of confidence or self-compassion?

• Are you consumed by negative emotions such as fear, anxiety, anger or resentment?

• Are you ready to change?

• Do you want change?

• Do you believe change is possible?

A great deal can depend on the power of your beliefs; if you think you can change you will, if you don't think you can, then you won't – it is completely up to you. This doesn't mean it's hard work, though, but it does take some awareness of the choices you are making, and enough respect for yourself to keep going.

Remember, this book focuses on how to grow your own happiness. These are things that need to be put into practice and applied to daily life. The idea is to keep going until it becomes effortless, until it has become a new way of being. In other words, until you create great new habits.

ACQUIRING NEW HABITS

Our current behaviour, especially if we have been repeating it for years, will have become a habit, whether it is a way of reacting to, thinking about or doing a certain thing. As we go from repeating old habits (point A), to acquiring new ones (point B), we are in transition. During this phase we need to be aware that we are breaking old habits and creating new ones. When we get to point B and our new behaviour has finally become habit, we will realize that we are automatically responding and reacting in ways that we have been striving for, with little or no conscious effort.

Sometimes we are so used to our ways of being that we don't even question them, we accept them as though we have no choice. "This is just the way I am" is a common phrase. However, we *do* have choice. We can change and we have the power to increase our life satisfaction.

WHAT IS YOUR MINDSET?

Part of knowing that greater happiness is possible comes from understanding the difference between having a *fixed mindset* or a *growth mindset*. Psychologist Carol Dweck coined the term "growth mindset" following years of research into understanding both ways of thinking. A person with a fixed mindset believes that character, intelligence and creativity are fixed, that they will not, or cannot, really change in any big way. A person with a fixed mindset often measures "success" with things such as academic achievements and awards. This leads to their self-esteem and self-worth going up or down as they fail or achieve these standards.

However, because their self-worth is so closely connected with success or failure, there is also likely to be a fear of failure, thus creating a potential barrier to learning and developing.

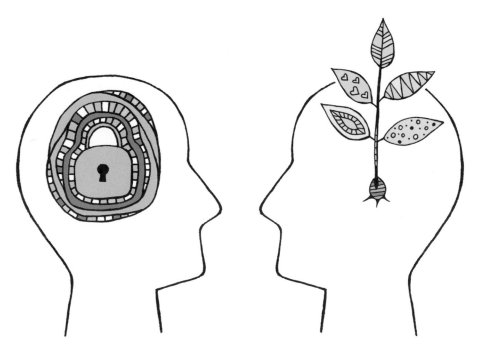

fixed mindset   growth mindset

Fear of failure holds back a person's desire to try something new, to step out of their comfort zone. The goal becomes about avoiding failure rather than learning something new and developing. This is particularly so if you see failure as a reflection of your lack of self-worth and you are trying to avoid all the unpleasant feelings that go with that feeling. We look at this more in the Relationships chapter (see page 178).

A person with a growth mindset enjoys learning and challenges, seeing "failure" as a sign that they need to develop and practise more to be able to "succeed". Failure to them is not an indication of their lack of intelligence and self-worth.

Growth-mindset people have a passion for learning and developing, whereas fixed-mindset people are prone to craving approval, resulting in a lifetime of trying to prove and validate themselves, which is exhausting and never-ending.

Dweck did a study with four-year-old children, who were given the choice to redo an easy puzzle or try a harder one. The children with the fixed mindset chose to redo the same puzzle, as they wanted to succeed in order to appear and/or feel smart, whereas the growth-mindset children chose the harder puzzle as they wanted to stretch themselves and become smarter.

LEARN FROM THE SETBACKS

It will come as no surprise when I say that breaking old habits and making new ones is not always a straight journey from A to B. In fact, more often than not, it is like a series of loops.

If you encounter setbacks while you are trying to break habits, it's important that you recognize that it is all part of learning and moving forward – it does not mean that you have "failed" and are back at the start.

Those setbacks can actually be good for you, as they can reinforce your learning, determination and resilience. If a journey is too easy, then we tend not to appreciate it or learn very much, as it does not set us up for using those skills in the future when life is difficult. Setbacks give us a sense of achievement that comes from conquering something difficult and moving forward, as opposed to repeating the same old patterns. So learn to welcome the challenges and take them on like the heroine or hero that you are!

Try It Out:
See for Yourself

Try the suggestions in this book for at least two months and then make your own judgement about whether they are beneficial to your life, health and relationships.

The Benefits of Happiness

Happiness is more than just feeling good, it has many beneficial consequences. Happiness can help improve:

Your physical health
- Lowers risk of heart disease by decreasing heart rate and blood pressure
- Strengthens the immune system
- Increases longevity

Your mental health
- Lowers stress levels
- Aids quicker recovery from stressful situations
- Counteracts negative emotions
- Increases resilience

Your relationships with others
- Improves friendships
- Helps build stronger relationships, partnerships or marriages
- Leads to better parenting

Your performance at work
- Increases productivity
- Improves chances of increasing sales
- Improves career opportunities and increased income

Your general wellbeing
- Increases creativity
- Creates a broader, more open mind
- Increases mental flexibility
- Helps maintain healthy behaviour
- Increases life satisfaction
- Improves optimism and hope
- Increases posititvity

My Path to Happiness

I was born and raised in West London. I had wonderful parents, whom I have always admired greatly – my mother has Indian heritage and my father was from East London. I also have an older brother; we are blessed to have such a close and loving family.

I was an independent and strong-minded child. When my mother decided to learn how to meditate to help ease her migraines, I also wanted to be taught, even though I was only six. My mother chose not to continue with her meditation at that time (she picked it up again years later), but I took it seriously and maintained my practice. I would take myself off to see the local meditation teacher on a regular basis (it was the 1970s – kids had a lot more freedom then).

At school I was quite rebellious, due to undiagnosed dyslexia and dyspraxia. Nobody, including myself, understood why I struggled with certain things when I was clearly intelligent (I was eventually diagnosed at 46, when I started my master's degree). Like a lot of people in my situation, I ended up misbehaving and was repeatedly asked to move on to another school. I left school at 15 with two O Levels and no respect for education. Unfortunately, the whole experience had a negative impact on my self-worth and self-esteem.

When I was 16, I wanted to learn meditation again, but this time as an 'adult'. I went to a local meditation class, which happened to be held at the London Buddhist Vihara. The monk who taught the class also talked about Buddhism, which sparked my interest in the subject. For the first time in my life, I wanted to study something, rather than have it imposed upon me. I took class after class and studied Buddhist philosophy and psychology at the Vihara. I couldn't get enough. I was amazed there was a philosophy that fitted with how I'd always thought and felt, and that had names for feelings I'd always had – it was like finding a place where everyone spoke the same language as you when your life up to that point had been lived in a strange land. I was so blessed to be taught by the most amazing monks, most of whom were from Sri Lanka.

I left home at 16 and worked during the day, but in the evenings and at weekends I was at the Vihara. I soon decided I wanted to take the robes and become a nun, but life had another plan for me – at 18 I discovered I was pregnant. This was something I was very happy about from the moment I found out and, without a shadow of a doubt, my son was and still is the best thing that has happened to me. He is my primary life meaning and motivation.

I couldn't afford to continue living in my flat and for months I tried to find somewhere else, but eventually I left with nowhere to go (unfortunately my parents had said no to me moving back home). Homeless and heavily pregnant, I was placed in a grimy B&B in the city – it was a tiny, dirty room with no cooking facilities and a shared bathroom down the hall. Luckily, just before my son was due to be born, I was moved to a women's hostel. It was still pretty depressing – the only window faced a brick wall – but at least I had an electric camping cooker and I managed to get a second-hand pram that would also serve as my son's cot.

A year later, we moved to another temporary accommodation, which seemed better, until one night a man tried to kick our door down as he screamed for someone and shouted that he was going to kill them (presumably he was looking for the person who lived there before me). I had to keep my baby quiet so that the man would think no one was in and go away. We stayed in this place for about nine months, until we were given a flat in a rough housing estate – the flat had become available because the council had evicted squatters the day before and had to have new occupants in place within 24 hours.

The flat was completely trashed. I didn't have any furniture or money, but I found stuff in skips or second-hand, and spent ages decorating and making it a home. We lived there for three years – it was a hard environment to be in, people were always screaming and shouting, sometimes getting stabbed or even shot. One night, two men were fighting outside our flat and one of them got pushed through the window. Some shards of shattered glass landed in my son's cot on the other side of the room, but luckily he wasn't in it.

I felt for the kids on the estate and used to invite them into our flat to play – it was nice to see them relax, even the older ones enjoyed playing. I don't think they ever got a chance to just be kids. When an opportunity to move to the Welsh mountains came up (after my grandfather died, my father bought a cottage for the family to use, and it was agreed that my son and I could live there as housekeepers), I struggled with whether I could leave those kids, as it didn't seem fair that we could leave and they couldn't. A friend of mine asked, "Do you think any of them would stay for you?" Ultimately, I knew I had to leave for my son's sake.

We moved to rural Wales a couple of months before my son's fourth birthday. I shall never forget him saying to me, "Mum, listen…" I asked him what I was listening for, as there literally wasn't a sound. He said, "There's no fighting here." It was exactly the environment I wanted him to grow up in. Peaceful, beautiful and in the middle of nature – he could go off exploring and be totally safe. However, what I didn't expect was the prejudice we received. It was a small Welsh-speaking farming community and I was a young English single mother from London. We didn't know anyone, and it was a shock to get such negative reactions.

There were still plenty of good times, though. One day, an English woman asked if I would teach meditation. I was nervous, but nonetheless I started teaching a weekly class. It was a lovely class and I am still friends with some of the people who used to come. I also completed a degree in psychology via The Open University, which entailed studying on my own, mostly at night, for six years. There was no internet yet at that time, and part of the course was delivered via programmes on the television and radio. Unfortunately, I couldn't receive either in the Welsh hills!

We lived in Wales for ten years, until my son reached adolescence. Living in the mountains no longer had the same appeal for him, so we moved to Bath, which was a great compromise – a beautiful small city with lovely countryside all around.

One of the difficulties I have repeatedly found myself dealing with over the course of my life is the death of a loved one, starting with a close friend who died in an accident when I was 16. It's always difficult to cope with, whatever the circumstances, but I think it's particularly difficult when the loss is unexpected. As anyone who has been through this experience will know, it is extremely painful and it takes time to recover. When my father died unexpectedly in 2012, I scaled down my clients, stopped the meditation classes I was teaching in Bath and enrolled for a master's degree in Positive Psychology. I wanted to make sure I did something productive with the time out I needed to take.

In 2014, while I was working towards my master's, I had the idea to incorporate wellbeing and Positive Psychology into the Weight Watchers (now known as WW) programme and had my first meeting with the organization's UK Vice President. I designed a programme with the premise "Happier people make healthier choices" and ran a workshop for the International Senior Executive team, who flew to the UK from various countries to attend. I worked with Weight Watchers throughout 2015, helping to run trials in the UK and US, training the UK trainers and area managers. The results were so positive that 18 months after my first meeting, the "Eat, Move, Smile" programme was launched in the UK – "Smile" being the wellbeing, Positive Psychology aspect.

It was the monks at the London Buddhist Vihara and my psychologist and mentor, Alex Barakan, who helped me have faith in myself. After studying Buddhism, I went on to study Western psychology, which enabled me to help and support others. Buddhism and psychology are still my two great passions, and throughout the years, my whole family has remained close to the Vihara. My mother goes there several times a week, my father helped design the shrine room when the Vihara moved to a new building and my son was given his middle name by the Venerable Dr Vajiragnana, the temple's head monk and the most senior Theravada Buddhist monk in the UK. The list of opportunities and experiences is incredibly long – my gratitude to the many monks at the Vihara is indescribable. It is no exaggeration to say they changed my life and I am, and will always be, deeply grateful to them all.

My life has changed enormously over the years, and I believe I have achieved post-traumatic growth. I know you can too. And in case you are wondering, my amazing son is doing brilliant things, helping people around the world and is based in Washington, DC.

CHAPTER **1**

Gratitude

We're often great at telling others when they've done something we don't like, moaning about a situation we're not happy with or pointing out people's failings. But we're not always so good at expressing gratitude, our appreciation to others or the world around us.

Yet we are aware of how it makes us feel when someone expresses their gratitude, shows their appreciation or says a heartfelt "thank you" to us. It makes us feel good, appreciated and recognized for what we've done.

Expressing gratitude starts with retraining our minds to be aware and notice different things. For example, when you are thinking about buying a certain new car, you start seeing that type of car on the road all the time. Of course, it's not that all of a sudden there are more of those particular cars around, but your awareness of them has heightened.

We can choose to notice the things we are not happy with and allow ourselves to feel more and more disgruntled with life. Or we can choose to notice the things we are thankful for and feel greater life satisfaction. The choice is ours.

Naturally, there needs to be a balance. I'm not saying you have to delude yourself or that you should ignore things that aren't right. As we will see later in the chapter on Positivity (see page 86), we do have a tendency toward negativity and therefore we need to be aware of that and mindfully compensate for it.

Ideally, we will be aware of the reality of any situation and, if there is a bias, then let it be toward the positive, so we can focus on the things we are grateful for within that situation.

Where is the Gratitude?

There is a lot more to gratitude than we may first think. My favourite definition is from one of the world's leading gratitude researchers, Robert Emmons, who defined gratitude as "a felt sense of wonder, thankfulness and appreciation for life."

As you can see from that definition, it is not simply about offering thanks to someone (although that is still important), it is an awareness of gratitude on a bigger scale. It is about shifting your mindset and having an appreciation for life.

We can experience a sense of awe when we look at the natural wonders of the world, for instance. But imagine what it would be like to experience that feeling more frequently, not just the handful of times you are lucky enough to chance across an amazing view.

There are so many situations where we could feel that sense of awe on a daily basis, if we just open our minds and hearts to them. The more you become aware, the more you will see. It opens a whole new level of awareness and positive feelings in your life and those around you. When you feel happier, so do those near to you – it's a win-win situation. This will be discussed further in the Relationships chapter (see page 178).

Try It Out: Think About Thanks

Pause now for a moment and think of a time when you felt a sense of awe, wonder and thankfulness. That moment could have been when you noticed a flower blooming in your garden, you went to a beautiful place on holiday, you looked up at the night sky full of stars, you held your newborn child or felt love for your pet. It might even have been listening to the sound of the birds singing in the morning.

Notice how you feel when you picture it or hear it clearly in your mind, how it shifts your mood. Write down how you feel. Now imagine how it would be to have that feeling on a regular basis – think about the impact on your life, your experience of life as a whole.

This exercise taps into something on a subtle level, an opening of the heart and mind, of your awareness, encouraging you to be mindful to all that is around you when that feeling could arise.

Try It Out:
Note It Down

Spend the day noting down the things you appreciate. This could be your comforting cup of tea or coffee, a lovely dinner, your partner, pet, health, home or your favourite song – the list is endless and so is the potential for feelings of gratitude.

It's Up to Us

We all have a choice about how we perceive the world, people and ourselves. We may feel as though we don't have a choice (and there will be times when we won't have much choice, if life or circumstances are too difficult). However, most of the time we have more control over our perception and reactions than we realize.

Think about how it makes you feel when someone expresses their appreciation for something that you've done for them. We feel good inside when our efforts are acknowledged. However, we probably didn't carry out the original deed in order to be appreciated, and so we may not mind if nothing is said once or twice. But if that lack of appreciation happens continually, we may get to a point where we don't want to carry on helping that person.

At this point it's common to feel upset at the lack of appreciation or recognition. We can feel we have been taken advantage of, the energy and time we have put in have not been valued. The end result can be that we don't want to do anything else for that person or organization – or even worse – for anyone ever again. In other words, we are left with a negative feeling that can be difficult to shift. However, if what we do is appreciated and acknowledged, then we feel good about what we have done and how we have helped another person.

Case Study:
No Thank You Very Much

I was visited by a couple who were coming to see me for couple's therapy. One of the pair hardly ever said thank you for anything – they never understood why it was important – and this had caused a rift in the relationship.

People's inability to see any value in expressing gratitude often reflects in their perception of life. For example, whenever the couple went somewhere, one of them would spend all their time pointing out flaws or failings of the place and the people. They spent their life complaining rather than seeing the good.

Feeling dissatisfied, rather than appreciating the effort people had put into something, they went around feeling like the victim, yet couldn't see that they were causing their own reality.

The way we perceive things affects the way we experience them. The couple would walk into the same place and one of them would think it was a beautiful place, full of people wanting to have a good time, and the other would be noticing the things that weren't perfect and harshly judging the people who were there.

I'm glad to say that in the end the particular individual began to shift their mindset and was a lot happier inside. The couple's relationship shifted too. They went from strength to strength and now they have a very loving relationship, full of mutual respect and appreciation.

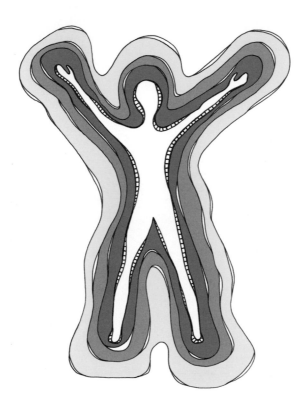

PASS IT ON

When we feel good we have a positive effect on those around us – it has a wonderful ripple effect on everything. We are also more likely to want to do something similar again for that person or group of people, as we were left with a positive feeling.

That is why people promote "random acts of kindness" – it makes you feel as good about sharing kindness as it does the person receiving it. Yet again it's a win-win situation – we want to reciprocate the feeling and it can boost our self-worth and self-esteem.

Think of a family or group of friends who all do favours for each other and the favours are recognized and appreciated. How strong are the bonds between that group of people? Decades of research have shown us that sharing kind favours strengthens us as a group.

SAYING NO TO YES

Do you find yourself always saying "Yes" to certain people when they ask for your help, because you fear it will damage your relationship with them if you say "No"? This is common, but there has to be a balance. It's important that when you give to others, you do not take away from yourself. This is where you need compassion for yourself, and how much you can reasonably do.

It also works the other way around – you need to have compassion for someone who says "No" to you, thinking about why they said "No" and why they might be unable to help.

The Effects of Gratitude

Research into the effects of gratitude shows that it can make people feel happier, more hopeful, optimistic, positive and satisfied with their lives. It is also known to be an antidote or neutralizer to negative emotions.

In other words, if you're feeling negative – angry, fearful, jealous or defensive, for example – then doing a gratitude exercise can help dissolve those feelings.

The effects can be seen on a physical level too. There is a difference in heart-rate variability between people who are thinking of things that make them angry compared to things that make them feel appreciative.

Try It Out:
Dissolve Anger

Take a moment to think of something that makes you angry and note down how you feel. Then think of something that makes you feel grateful – linger on that sense of gratitude for a while. Now see what that does to the anger and all the feelings associated with the anger. What emotion are you left with? How did your feelings change?

Case Study:
A Family Full of Thanks

After attending one of my workshops, Sarah (not her real name) realized she and her husband and two kids were wasting every Sunday by being unhappy. They arrived at their caravan every Friday and loved it, but on Sundays they spent all their time thinking about having to leave and how it would be a week until they were back again. It then hit her that they were wasting nearly half their precious weekends being miserable.

Sarah then explained to her family what she had learned about the power of gratitude, and shifting focus away from the negative (and what hadn't even happened yet), on to what was happening at that moment and what they appreciated. She told me how this had transformed their family life – not only do they now enjoy every Sunday, but they also keep a family gratitude journal and all enjoy writing in it.

The entire family's mindset has shifted to tune into what they are grateful for and the kids get excited when something happens that they want to write about in the gratitude journal. Sarah said the difference to the happiness and enjoyment of life for herself and her whole family has been amazing, "It's almost like we are two different families, one before the workshop and one after!"

See the Change

Changes are taking place within us all the time, and we do not always notice them. However, we may only become aware when the emotions swing to an extreme – that is, if we become really angry or really joyful.

More often than not, we are oblivious to our raised blood pressure, stress levels and tension in the body, for example. This means we can be equally unaware of the effect those negative states have on our bodies, relationships and life. Often it isn't until something dramatic happens that we become aware, by which time it takes a lot more effort to make changes.

There is nothing more powerful than your own experience to help you maintain a new behaviour and let it become a natural part of your way of being.

Once it does become a part of who you are, then it takes no effort at all; it will just be automatic. The journey from A to B, however, requires a little effort. It's a bit like wanting to go to a concert some distance away. You may know the route, you may know why it'll be good for you to go, and loads of people have told you how much fun it is. But you need to put the effort into driving all the way there – you can't stop part of the way and go back home, saying it was rubbish!

The Gratitude Measure

Take this test to get an understanding of your current levels of gratitude.

Below are some statements about gratitude. Note down how much you agree or disagree with each one, according to the scale below.

THE STATEMENTS:

A I feel grateful for something, or thankful to someone, several times a week, sometimes even a few times a day.

B There are many people in my life, both past and present, that I feel gratitude towards.

C I am grateful for what I do have in my life.

D I feel a sense of gratitude towards my physical body and my mind.

E I see so many things that inspire gratitude, a sense of awe or an appreciation for life as I look at the world.

F There is a lot in my life to be grateful for.

G As I reflect on years gone by I am able to appreciate the people and events that have formed the tapestry of my life.

Almost never feel this	Neutral	Almost always feel this

1	2	3	4	5

Now add up all the scores to give yourself an overall measure of gratitude.

Interpreting Your Score on the Gratitude Measure

Between 7 and 16
This low score may reflect how you are feeling right now and what is going on in your life. Naturally, there are times in life when it is hard to feel gratitude. When you are ready, you could begin to cultivate and grow your gratitude, which will have a positive effect on your life.

- *Begin to let the wonders of gratitude come into your life more – start by practising Level 1 of the Gratitude Journal exercise (see page 52).*

Between 17 and 26
This score indicates that you are just beginning to open up to the power of gratitude. You are going to really enjoy the changes in perspective that come as a result of the exercises on the following pages – it is exciting to be at the start of the gratitude experience.

- *Develop the mindset you already have by becoming more sensitive to gratitude – try Level 1 of the Gratitude Journal exercise (see page 52), followed by Level 2.*

Between 27 and 35
This score indicates that you are well aware of the power of gratitude – you are liable to feel it in most, if not all, areas of your life. Challenge yourself to find the things you can feel grateful for when life is difficult.

- *Take your levels of gratitude even further by trying the Gratitude Reflections exercise (see page 54), followed by the Gratitude Letter (see page 56). Have fun with the Pay It Forward exercise (see page 55).*

Exercises for Gratitude

Through my work, I have seen these exercises create amazing changes in countless clients, as well as within myself – they can make a profound difference to people's lives. Have fun trying all the different exercises; these are designed to be enjoyable, not a chore.

I use the term "gratitude" but you can replace it with whatever word is right for you – "appreciation", "sense of wonder", "thankfulness" or "awe". The important thing is the feeling, not the word. There will be gratitude toward others for something they have done, as well as gratitude toward people, animals and things simply for their existence.

No matter what level you are at on the Gratitude Measure, I would recommend trying the Expressing Gratitude and Pay It Forward exercises (see pages 53 and 55). It's interesting to do all these exercises for a while then come back to them in six months to see if there are any differences in your experience the second time around.

EXERCISE 1: GROWING GRATITUDE –
THE GRATITUDE JOURNAL

Level 1 – Starter

This is a great exercise for developing your awareness of all the things in your life for which you can be grateful.

• *Twice a week, write down three things that you have felt grateful for, since you did the last journal entry. I recommend doing this exercise for a minimum of one month.*

It can be anything at all but try not to repeat things. If you want to repeat something, try to find something particular about it. For example, if you're saying you're grateful for your child, then think of something specific about them or what they've done. We often start with the more obvious and, as we progress, it becomes more subtle as our awareness grows.

Level 2 – Deepening

This part should be done after Level 1, as it helps deepen your levels of gratitude. Having written the three things for which you are grateful, go one stage further by writing down what it was about that experience that made you grateful and how it made you feel. What enabled it? Was anyone else involved and, if so, how did their involvement affect the situation? What does it mean to you? Did you tell anyone about it? Did you acknowledge it to yourself at the time?

EXERCISE 2: EXPRESSING GRATITUDE

The way we express gratitude toward others makes a difference to how it is received. There are times when a simple thanks is right, but there are other times when more acknowledgement is appropriate.

There are three ways to offer thanks:

• *To acknowledge what the person has done for you, as you would normally*

• *To say how it made you feel when they did it*

• *To recognize and acknowledge what it took for them to do it*

The second and third are important. Think about when you last did something for someone and how you might have felt if they not only said thanks, but told you how it made them feel and acknowledged what it took for you to do it.

Friction in relationships can happen when these last two ways are neglected. This is because people often make the mistake of assuming you know how they feel and, of course, vice versa. It's best not to assume but to say, even if the person responds by saying, "You didn't need to say that". (Why people respond that way is a whole different story, which will have to wait for another book.)

EXERCISE 3: GRATITUDE REFLECTIONS

Reflecting on the past can be a positive exercise. Think back to people who have helped you through the years, think about what they did for you that helped. How have those things shaped you and how have they enabled you to be where you are now in your life?

• *Write down these recollections.*

They could be big things, which have had a huge impact, but they could also be small things, perhaps a comment the other person doesn't even remember saying. The important thing is to reflect on the various people and things that have had a positive impact on your life. Let that sense of gratitude emerge as you think and write about them.

• *Write down things that have happened that you initially thought were bad but later realized were a blessing in disguise.*

It is often surprising how, when we reflect on something that seemed terrible at the time, we see it was actually, in retrospect, a good thing. For example, not getting a job you desperately wanted but then a better opportunity arose, which you couldn't have taken if you had got the original job. We can often be quick to assume something is bad news, but we can't really make that judgement until we know the next sequence of events.

EXERCISE 4: PAY IT FORWARD (PiF)

This gratitude exercise is fun to do and, like all the others, leaves you feeling great. Having done the other exercises and been reminded of all the amazing things people have done for you, it's good to be able to do things for others too.

- *You might be inspired by recalling what someone did for you years ago – such as a teacher or neighbour who went out of their way for you – and you may want to do something similar yourself (see page 218 for a list of suggested voluntary organizations)..*

- *Often PiF is when you do something for a complete stranger, such as giving a homeless person a sandwich, paying for a coffee for the person behind you in the queue, helping an elderly person or doing some volunteer work.*

There is a lot of fun and joy to be had doing lovely things for others, especially when they don't expect it.

EXERCISE 5: GRATITUDE LETTER

Having done the Gratitude Reflections exercise and remembered the people who have done wonderful things for you in your life, choose one person to whom to write a gratitude letter.

Take your time, this mustn't be done in a hurry. When you have the time to write it, your emotions will flow naturally on to the page. It's not something that is carefully scripted, it's a flow of consciousness from your heart to theirs.

• *Don't think too much about it, just start writing and let it come.*

Once you've written it, the most powerful way to deliver it is by going to see the person and reading it to them. However, if that's not possible then send it to them, no matter how much time has gone by. It will mean a huge amount to the recipient, so do send it.

If the person has died then you can still send it to them. You can sit and bring them to mind and then read it to them. Alternatively, you could burn the letter and see the smoke as taking your message to them wherever they are. Even if the person died decades ago, trust me you will be glad you did this exercise, it is very powerful.

The Top Benefits of Gratitude

With more gratitude in your life, you will notice:

- Greater happiness
- Greater optimism
- More hope
- Stronger relationships
- Better social bonds
- Increased life satisfaction
- A more positive perception of the world
- You have an antidote to negative emotions
- Physical benefits, for example, reduced stress and heart-rate variability

CHAPTER 2

Mindfulness

Mindfulness is an increasingly popular practice used to improve wellbeing in a number of different ways. In its contemporary sense, mindfulness can be defined as "paying attention in a particular way – on purpose, in the present moment, and non-judgementally". In other words, there are three things to consider when paying attention:

On purpose – paying attention intentionally. For example, when you're walking through the countryside and you decide to be mindful, you may stop for a moment to mentally get yourself into a "mindful mode". You tell yourself that for the rest of the walk you are going to be fully aware of yourself and your environment. This is a conscious decision that is *on purpose* and with intention.

In the present moment Before you practise mindfulness, you might say that you're always in the present. However, we usually spend more time mentally in the past or future than in the present. It is surprisingly difficult to hold your mind in the present moment, to be present and aware in the here and now.

Non-judgementally This is about letting go of the millions of judgements we make about ourselves, others and the things around us.

So mindfulness is really about being able to be mindful; in other words, to be aware and fully conscious of the moment we are in. We miss a lot of life by not being present in the present. Practising mindfulness can help us both physically and psychologically. It will also support and encourage *all* the happiness practices that are discussed in this book.

The Benefits of Mindfulness

There are many physical, psychological and neuroscientific studies that show the effectiveness of mindfulness and meditation. Some of these benefits include:

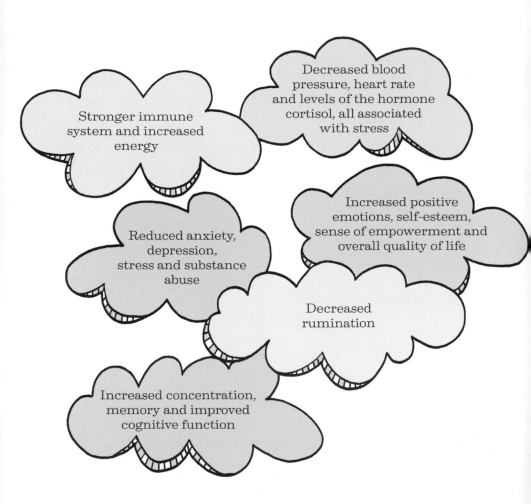

Stronger immune system and increased energy

Decreased blood pressure, heart rate and levels of the hormone cortisol, all associated with stress

Reduced anxiety, depression, stress and substance abuse

Increased positive emotions, self-esteem, sense of empowerment and overall quality of life

Decreased rumination

Increased concentration, memory and improved cognitive function

Research undertaken at the University of Massachusetts Medical School showed that physical changes become evident in the brain after only eight weeks of practising mindfulness. These changes occur in the areas of the brain involved in:

- Mind-wandering and emotion regulation
- Learning and memory
- Perspective-taking, empathy and compassion

These are all crucial factors for our wellbeing, as we now know that a wandering mind is an unhappy mind. Emotion regulation is an important aspect to wellbeing and mental health, while learning and memory are obviously important in many areas throughout life. Lastly, our ability to see things from various perspectives is beneficial to the way we experience and interpret the world and other people around us. Sometimes we can get stuck in our own perception of the world and struggle to understand how others are perceiving things.

This ability to take another perspective improves our relationships with others and with the world as a whole. If a person is stuck thinking that the whole world is against them, they can perceive everyone's behaviour in that way – this is a very unhappy and isolating place to be. However, if they have the ability to understand different perspectives, they find it easier to connect and empathize with others, which will result in a happier, more socially connected life.

More empathy and compassion can come from shifting perspectives and these two things really are key to our wellbeing – I will discuss this in more detail in the Relationships chapter (see page 178).

The changes in the brain of those who practised mindfulness for eight weeks were supported by blood tests, which showed a reduction in levels of the stress hormone cortisol. The participants of the study reported (without having been aware of the changes in brain structure or cortisol levels) that they felt less stressed and less anxious and experienced fewer instances of their mind wandering. They also reported an increase in their quality of life. The great thing about this study is the fact that the changes that were measured in the brain, blood and in the participants' reports all support each other by coming to the same conclusion. And all this in only eight weeks – imagine how you could feel if mindfulness became part of your everyday life.

NEUROPLASTICITY – A TIME FOR CHANGE

We now know the brain, like every other muscle in our body, can be worked on and developed – this is what is known as *neuroplasticity*. We used to think that brain structure didn't change once we reached adulthood, other than to decline with age, but that thinking has now changed.

The amygdala is a key part of the brain which can be developed by practising mindfulness. The amygdala is commonly known as our fear centre, and is crucial to our stress and anxiety response. After eight weeks practising mindfulness, the amygdala is seen to shrink and people feel less stressed and anxious.

How Does Neuroplasticity Work?

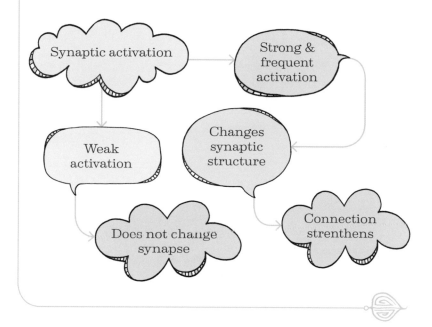

In other words, the more you think, or do, something the more you affect particular corresponding parts of the brain. You need to be aware how you are affecting your brain and make a conscious choice to affect it in a positive way.

Where's Your Head At?

The more you are in the present – known as *the experiential mode* – the less you are stuck in your head, in the noisy *narrative mode*. People with depression, anxiety and stress often get stuck in the narrative mode. Being in the here and now results in feeling more relaxed, happy, positive and creative.

For example, we can spend weeks or months before a holiday dreaming of relaxing on the beach and having a break from work and life's other stresses. But when we're finally lying on the beach, we can end up not being present at all, as we are still worrying about work issues or personal stresses. This means, in effect, we end up missing the holiday we've been so looking forward to.

In fact, we often do this in all sorts of situations – at our child's birthday party, for example, we can miss the entire thing when we're stressing about something that has already happened, or could potentially happen. This lack of mindfulness can have some significant consequences as we miss special times in life, or just life generally. If we are able to be mindful, we will increase our enjoyment of life as a whole and even the seemingly mundane moments will become pleasurable.

Naturally, there are times when we need to think about the past or the future. Thinking of the past can help us to learn from it, which is a positive thing. But this is very different from thinking of the past and ruminating,

Be Here Now

Think about how much of your day you spend actually in the present moment, not ruminating over the past or thinking about the future, but really in the *now*.

Try monitoring this for a day, or even an hour, and make a note of how much you're in the past, future and present. It is likely you will lean more toward either the past or the future (rarely the present), which in itself will give you an insight into yourself.

dwelling and/or criticizing ourselves. Similarly, thinking of the future can be positive as it allows us to plan. Positive planning is very different from stressing and being anxious about future events. The important thing is to get the balance right and be able consciously to choose which you are thinking about. Mindfulness and meditation enable you to become the master of your own mind, rather than feeling that your thoughts and emotions are controlling you and that you are powerless over them.

Take your attention into yourself now, for a moment – what do you notice? Your breath, your physical posture, noises around you, the feeling of your clothes on your body, your feet touching the ground. Punctuate your day with mindful moments like this, as they will help to bring you into the now.

Try It Out: Walk with Awareness

Next time you are walking – whether it's a country walk or just walking to the local shop – start by tuning in to what's going on in your mind. Is your mind full of stuff, such as worries, stresses, plans, the past or future, or is it quiet and just noticing the things around you – the trees, the flowers, the weather, people and so on?

We can start by being aware of what is going on in our minds and then choose what we want to do with it. If it's full of thoughts unrelated to what's going on in the present moment, then you may choose to let it go and focus on what is in the now.

Notice how you are feeling, physically and mentally. For example, are you feeling happy and relaxed? Stressed or anxious? Are you holding any tension in your body? It's important to be as aware as possible.

Meditate to Be Mindful

Meditation is what enables mindfulness, and it is very difficult to practise mindfulness without first having practised meditation.

Meditation is where you learn how to observe the self, not be distracted and let go of judgement. The more you practise meditation, the easier it is to have mindfulness naturally, as it will come as a consequence of your practice.

There are many guided meditations available online or as apps. It's best for beginners to start with a short meditation of around two minutes, before trying a longer practice. This makes it manageable and sustainable, and easier to integrate into daily life. It is better to have a good five-minute meditation every day than a mediocre 45-minute meditation once a week.

Think of meditation like polishing silver, with silver representing the mind. When silver hasn't been polished for a long time it turns dull and black, as does the mind without meditation. It then takes a lot of polishing to get it back to its original shining state. Once the silver is shiny, you only have to polish it briefly to keep it that way. Similarly, when you start meditating it may take a while to get a shiny mind – but once you have, a brief, but regular, practice will keep that mind shining.

Meditation will help you take care of your mind. If you think about the time we spend every day taking care of our bodies, teeth, hair and so on, it's amazing to think we rarely spend time on our brain – the very thing that controls our whole system.

BREATHING AND COMPASSION

Breathing Meditation (see page 68) is the best meditation to start with and important to maintain no matter how long you've been a meditator. It helps to develop your concentration, so it is your foundation for other meditations. When you are comfortable with the Breathing Meditation, you can try the Compassion Meditation (see page 69).

When you feel you have developed a sense of compassion and empathy toward yourself, then you can start sending it out to other people (anticipate spending at least six months developing it toward yourself before sending it out to others).

To do this, start by directing the phrases toward yourself and then direct them toward your closest loved ones, to family and friends, work colleagues, neighbours and, finally, toward anyone you have bad feelings toward. This will be discussed further in the Relationships chapter (see page 178).

In other words, you start by sending it toward people to whom you already feel compassion and empathy, ending up with people who you find more challenging. It's good to be aware of whatever feelings and emotions arise as you go through this – it can be difficult, but it is extremely beneficial to yourself and those around you. You will find it positively changes your relationship with yourself, as well as others.

Try It Out: Breathing Meditation

The breath is a convenient thing to focus your attention on – it's not about the breath itself, more a way to help you focus. It's like a post where you can tether a pet dog – the post is the breath and the dog is your mind. The idea is to find a point where you can hold your attention on the breath – either the stomach rising and falling, or the feeling of the air at the edge of the nostrils, or on the upper lip. Then just be aware as you breathe in and out – not trying to control it in any way, simply noticing what is, such as whether the breath is long or short.

Each time your mind wanders, which it *will*, you can gently bring it back to the breath. Counting is a great way to hold the focus – counting one as you breathe in, two as you breathe out, and so on up to ten. Then repeat, from one to ten. You may find that you go beyond ten, get lost in thought and forget that you were meant to be meditating – when you realize, just bring your mind back to the breath and start again at one.

By repeatedly bringing the mind back and starting again at one, you will find you slowly begin to hold your focus for longer and longer periods – hence your ability to be mindful outside meditation will also improve. After you have been practising for a while, you may want to let go of the counting, and that is fine. Counting is like a banister – it's helpful to hold on to, but after a while you are happy to let go. You can find guided breathing meditations of different lengths online.

Once you get used to meditating on a regular basis – ideally daily but at least several times a week – you will be aware that your meditation reflects what is going on in your life. If life is calm then your meditation will be too, and when life is difficult your meditation will be disturbed. At more turbulent times it's helpful to bring in the counting again to stabilize you through difficult days.

Try It Out: Compassion Meditation

Compassion Meditation, traditionally known as Loving Kindness Meditation, is a lovely practice that helps develop compassion and empathy toward ourselves and others. Any meditation is an act of kindness toward yourself and others, but Compassion Meditation takes that to another level. With this meditation, the focus is on a series of words which you repeat slowly in your mind.

As you say the words to yourself in the meditation, be mindful of any emotions that arise. They are not always the emotions you might expect. Sometimes people feel the opposite emotions to the ones they are saying.

There can be a lot of subconscious resistance to this meditation, depending on the way you feel about yourself and how comfortable you are having a compassionate, empathetic mind toward yourself.

Repeat these words in your mind for ten minutes:

I am happy

I am healthy

I recognize and appreciate who I am

I have inner confidence

I am joyful

I am peaceful

When you have completed your meditation, finish with the phrase:

May all beings be well, happy and peaceful.

POSITIVITY RISING

As we will see in the chapter on Positivity (see page 86), positive emotions build personal "resources" – as people's positive emotions increase, so do personal factors such as their purpose in life, life satisfaction and self-acceptance.

Research shows that Compassion Meditation increases your social connectedness and positivity toward other people. It also increases positive emotions. In fact, research in Detroit has shown that participants who practised Compassion Meditation for seven weeks experienced a significant increase in positive emotions during the study. The more the (mostly novice) meditators in the study practised, the more their positive emotions increased. This was an observable difference from the beginning to the end of the seven weeks. The positive emotions measured were amusement, awe, contentment, joy, gratitude, hope, interest, love and pride.

Other than discussing the results of practising meditation and mindfulness (which often helps motivate people to stick with the practice), I am always reluctant to say too much about what may (or may not) happen within meditation, as that can prevent the practice from developing naturally. Because we are all individuals, each of us will have slightly different experiences and will develop in different ways and at different speeds.

The important thing is that it happens naturally for *you*. Problems can arise when people have expectations about what they think should happen, which can obscure what is actually happening.

ENLISTING HELP

It's a good idea to find a meditation teacher who can give you guidance and whom you can ask questions. You will then be guided on your journey as you practise.

There are many different types of meditation, which are suitable for different people and at different times. Ideally, your meditation teacher will advise on what is right for you. Both the Breathing Meditation and Compassion Meditation in this book are suitable for the majority of people most of the time.

Over time, as your level of concentration increases, you will be able to practise more advanced meditations which require extra awareness. It is important to build up your concentration first, which will come with the Breathing Meditation, as it is easy to become lost in some meditations and achieve very little.

Exceptions to the Rule

Of course, there are always exceptions to every rule and there have been some reports of people having bad experiences with mindfulness. In general, I would say it is best to avoid practising mindfulness and meditation if you are experiencing a major depressive episode or have any other clinically diagnosed psychiatric illness, such as psychosis or bipolar disorder.

If you are extremely stressed or anxious, meditation can feel as though it is making matters worse, as thoughts and feelings can seem overwhelming. It is always best to ask the advice of your doctor, psychologist or counsellor. Ideally, mindfulness and meditation is a skill to be developed when you are feeling relatively OK, as it will then enable you to cope more effectively in difficult periods.

Try It Out:
Gently Does It

Try to let go of your mind's chatter and fully embrace the moment – see how long you can hold your mindfulness. Each time your mind wanders on to other things, you may find it helpful to say to yourself in a gentle tone, "Just be here now".

Teaching and training the mind is like teaching a child or training a pet – it takes lots of patience as you gently bring them back to what you want them to do. Nothing will be achieved if there is any irritation, frustration or anger.

Weeding the Garden of Your Mind

Unhelpful thoughts are like weeds – they begin small and can be easily pulled up, but if you leave them, they can quickly take over your garden and become difficult to uproot. The more you practise mindfulness, the more you will see those small weeds taking root, giving you the choice of whether to uproot them or not. When thoughts arise in the mind, try to be aware of them and notice whether they are weeds or, in fact, flowers which you want to allow to bloom.

JUDGEMENT DAZE

As discussed earlier in the book, our feelings will affect our thoughts and our thoughts will affect our feelings. It is a two-way system. The more we become aware of how we feel and what we are thinking, the more choice we have. Meditation teaches us how to control our thoughts, so once we know what we are thinking, we have the opportunity to direct our thoughts in a helpful, positive direction.

Negative emotions can arise due to judgement – if we accept that our minds have been allowed to jump around for our entire lives and, for the first time, we are now trying to control them, then we will be more patient and understanding with ourselves.

Judgement arises from not accepting the way things are. For example, if our minds keep wandering and are difficult to control, our judgement might tell us that we *should* be able to focus, or that we *shouldn't* stress about a conversation we had yesterday, or that we *should* be enjoying our walk, and so it goes on.

It's amazing how judgemental we are toward ourselves. We often speak to ourselves with a harsh, negative inner voice, yet we would never say those same things to our best friends. So why do we think it's OK to say these things to ourselves? Quite simply, it's not OK. I will talk more about our relationships with ourselves in the Relationships chapter (see page 178).

Being Mindful of Our Judgement

Being judgemental can be so ingrained in us that it's easy to make judgements without even realizing we are doing so. The moment we meet a new person we will make a judgement, or sometimes we will judge someone we pass in the street, even if we know nothing about them – this indicates that our judgement is often based on superficial things. Even when we know someone fairly well, we are still unlikely to know exactly what is going on for that person. The more mindful we become of judgements, the more we will realize we are judgemental about a lot of things – we have ideas, opinions, we like this, we don't like that and so it goes on.

It's not always so easy to be non-judgemental, but the more mindful we are, the more we give ourselves the opportunity to challenge our own judgements, rather than blindly believe them. I believe that when we judge ourselves and others, it comes from a lack of understanding – the more we understand ourselves or the other person, the less likely we are to judge them. Ultimately, we will want to rise above those judgements, to free ourselves from that simplistic black-and-white thinking, in order to free ourselves from the small-mindedness that comes with being judgemental.

Space to Be Mindful

Mindfulness creates a space between feelings, thoughts and reactions. It is within those spaces that we have the ability to choose the most appropriate reaction – that is, to have an intelligent and conscious response.

It gives us enough time to think about what we want to do in response to the thoughts and feelings, rather than get overtaken, consumed or caught up by them, therefore potentially reacting in ways we later regret.

Intelligent action comes when we see the space in between being stimulated, the emotion arising and our response to that emotion. We can then make a conscious, mindful choice about how we respond.

A classic example is having an argument with someone. Often people get so caught up in how they are feeling that they say and do things they later regret, sometimes severely damaging their relationship. When there are spaces in between, we have the ability to recognize that "there is anger", begin to detach from it and therefore respond in a more mindful way – even if that means you have to say you need five minutes to be able to respond in a helpful, as opposed to a harmful, way.

It takes time to see that space, and it takes practice to not just mindlessly react but to react mindfully. We can then take responsibility for our actions rather than say or think, "I couldn't help it, I was angry" or "I didn't mean what I said, I was upset".

MINDFULNESS CREATES SPACE

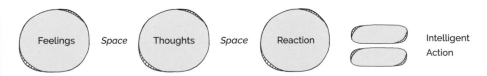

Feelings *Space* Thoughts *Space* Reaction   Intelligent Action

On Automatic

You can do any task mindfully. It's amazing how, when we start being mindful, we realize just how much we are on automatic pilot; we do a task but our minds are on other things.

When we are learning something new, our mindfulness is much sharper, but once we've learned how to do it, or become accustomed to it, our minds tend to drift. Driving is a classic example. If you are a driver, I'm sure you can remember what it was like to learn how to drive – it seemed like there were so many things to remember at the same time – clutch, gears, checking mirrors, looking at the road, other drivers, pedestrians and cyclists. When you start learning, it can feel like an impossible task, but once you've been driving for a few years it becomes completely automatic and your mind tends to go elsewhere.

Mindfulness is important in everyday moments as it helps us get out of automatic pilot and back into being fully aware, the same way as when we first learn something. Other times when that level of mindfulness arises naturally is when you are totally absorbed in doing something that you love. This often happens when you do something artistic, such as painting, drawing, knitting, writing or playing an instrument. You can lose all sense of time, as you are totally focused on what you are doing. The next time that happens, notice how you felt before and after the activity. Did your stress level drop? Did you feel happier, lighter, more relaxed afterward?

Beginner's or Child's Mind

A beginner, or child, will approach even the most mundane things with interest and curiosity. Children can react with great enthusiasm and excitement in a way that adults often don't. If we can train ourselves to see the world with a child's eyes then we are more likely to feel the sense of awe and gratitude that was discussed in the Gratitude chapter. If we imagine it is the first time we are seeing or experiencing something, our senses will be heightened and our appreciation and gratitude will increase, as will our enjoyment.

MAKING TIME FOR MINDFULNESS

A comment I often hear is, "I haven't got any time in my day to practise mindfulness – I have to multitask otherwise I wouldn't get everything done." Multitasking is a myth! We think we are able to multitask but actually our minds can only hold one thought at a time. Our minds appear to be doing more because they jump so rapidly from one thought to the next. Linda Stone coined the term Continuous Partial Attention which I think describes it perfectly.

If we stopped trying to multitask we would be more efficient. We would also feel less stressed as we are not putting that pressure on ourselves and expecting our brains to do something they can't do.

Mindful Eating

The wonderful thing about mindfulness is that it's portable. You can raise your level of awareness wherever you are, whether that's on the bus, train, walking or sitting in your garden. Mindful eating is another great way to bring mindfulness into everyday life. There are five different aspects of mindful eating to think about:

1. Mindful awareness vs mindless eating

How much of what you consume is consumed mindlessly? For example, do you open a bag of potato chips and enjoy the first one, then eat the rest of the bag almost without noticing until you get to the last few chips, and then you savour those?

This is a common pattern – to register and enjoy the first and last mouthful, bite or sip of something. I remember one man saying to me, after practising mindful eating for a week, "I notice everything on my plate now, whereas before I would have just 'inhaled' the food!"

2. Non-judgemental attitude vs guilty thoughts

How often do you eat something and then feel guilty? This is a destructive pattern and usually results in eating more, not less.

As I mentioned earlier, it's important to develop a non-judgemental attitude toward yourself, as this is a more positive and beneficial mindset. It also means that when you do decide to eat something that might have previously caused you to feel guilty, you are able to enjoy and savour it, rather than have a horrible aftertaste of guilt.

3. Savour the taste, smell, texture and look of the food or drink

If we eat mindfully, our enjoyment and appreciation of what we consume increase. It's like turning up the volume on all our senses.

Enjoyment of food starts with the look of it, then we appreciate the way it smells and finally the way it tastes. But to *really* appreciate all these things, we need to eat slowly with total awareness. Slow enough to really savour every mouthful.

4. Be in the moment – turn off the screens

To be able to eat mindfully we need to have no distractions. It is common for people to eat in front of a screen – be that the TV, a laptop or scrolling through their phone. This means there is little or no awareness of what you are consuming. In other words, it's time to turn everything off and be in the moment.

5. Be mindful of your emotions

If you tend to eat when you are upset, stressed, depressed or tired, ask yourself if you are hungry or if you want to eat because of how you are feeling? It is common to eat due to an emotional, not a physical need. Be careful not to "eat" your emotions – find a way to express and release them instead of pushing them down.

The more mindful you are, the more you will be able to respond appropriately to your mental and physical needs. Not only will this help before you consume anything, but it will also help afterward as you become more aware of how you react to different things. You will soon notice what makes you feel good and what doesn't.

Try It Out: Eating Mindfully

I suggest trying this exercise with fruit – a strawberry, a segment of orange or a single raisin are ideal.

- Start by observing. Look at the colour, the shape, the texture. Maybe you start noticing things about it you've never noticed before – if it's soft or hard, for instance.

- Notice how you feel. Are you looking forward to eating it? Has your mouth started watering? Enjoyment of food usually starts the moment we see it, before we've even tasted it.

- Be aware of the scent. How does the smell of the food make you feel? Does it make you want to eat it even more?

- Think of where the food has come from. Is it natural? Has it been processed? Think of the journey the food has taken to get to you.

- Place the food into your mouth. Chew it slowly, notice what you are tasting, the flavours – is it sweet or bitter, is it juicy? What is the texture like? Notice your reaction as you put it into your mouth and as you chew it.

- Notice if it's easy (or difficult) to eat slowly and mindfully. Do you normally rush when eating or do you savour the food?

- Notice how you feel when you've eaten it. What emotions and physical feelings do you have? Are you happy or guilty? Are you satiated or bloated?

- Be present with each piece of food. Really enjoy what you're eating – the look, the smell and the flavour, and how it makes you feel afterward.

- Does this experience differ from how you normally eat? What were you aware of? How did it make you feel? How did it affect your taste, enjoyment and ability to savour and appreciate the food?

Case Study:
The Chocoholic

Mindful eating has an added benefit if you are trying to lose weight and/or eat more healthily. I've had positive results with my research on mindfulness, helping people to lose weight and have a more positive relationship with food and themselves.

One story that always makes me smile involves a lady who was stunned at her experience of mindful eating. She explained that she had always been a "chocoholic", something her family and friends were aware of as she had a reputation for it. But when she practised mindful eating, and mindfully ate a piece of chocolate, she was horrified to discover she didn't like it! She found it was too sweet and she hated the texture in her mouth. She was even more astonished to find that she enjoyed eating fruit (something she had to force herself to do before) more than chocolate when she ate mindfully.

Use Your Senses

After you have tried the mindful eating exercise on page 80, try to use this level of mindfulness whenever you do everyday things, such as brushing your teeth, doing the washing up or walking to work. Try to be aware of whatever arises, allow nothing to be a distraction, and everything to be just as it is. And remember, it's not just taste – your other senses can be used as objects of attention, too. For instance:

Hearing – particularly nice when you're out in nature – listen to the sound of birds, water, leaves in the trees.

Smelling – again I would recommend trying when you're in nature – try to smell the rain or freshly cut grass, or think about what you can smell when out for a walk in the forest or visiting the coast.

Touching – really notice the feel of different textures, physical touch with other people, the feel of stroking animals, or heat and cold against your skin when outside.

Seeing – narrow your focus to limit an overload of visual information. Try focusing on a candle or a flower.

The possibilities with mindfulness are endless and the more you develop it, the more you will appreciate your life and all that is within it, while reconnecting with your authentic self.

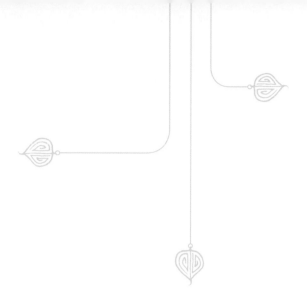

Mindfulness Shared

Mindfulness has become more and more recognized over the past few years, and as the scientific evidence relating to its effectiveness increases, so does the popularity of the practice.

The practice of mindfulness can be found in many places, from hospitals to multinational corporations such as Google and Facebook, as well as in schools all around the world. The popularity of the practice has also made it more accepted in Western societies. Sally Boyle, the head of Human Capital Management at Goldman Sachs, illustrated this point when she said, "In years to come we'll be talking about mindfulness as we talk about exercise."

The acceptance and understanding of mindfulness over the past 25 years has been enormous. It has shifted from being seen as an eccentric practice and made its way into the mainstream. When I began teaching mindfulness more than 25 years ago, one woman asked me if the classes were like aerobics! That shows the level of misunderstanding there was about it then, compared to now when it has become part of everyday language.

Jon Kabat-Zinn

We must give credit to the American professor Jon Kabat-Zinn for his role in the shift in understanding mindfulness, as well as the fact it is now being practised in such a wide variety of environments. Kabat-Zinn first applied mindfulness to outpatients in a stress-reduction clinic in Massachusetts.

Mindfulness has its roots in Buddhism, which is how Kabat-Zinn first came to learn it. My background is also in Buddhism, although there is no need to be Buddhist to either practise mindfulness, or to benefit from it. In fact, Kabat-Zinn removed the religious aspects from it to make it accessible to all.

However, Kabat-Zinn does discuss the need to keep the substance of the Buddha's teaching within mindfulness, especially for those who teach it. He stresses the importance of how mindfulness teachers need to have an in-depth knowledge and experience of Buddhist meditation.

The Top Benefits of Mindfulness

Thousands of studies have explored and indicated the effectiveness of mindfulness on physical, psychological and neuroscientific levels. In fact, the list of benefits is so long that I only have space to list the main ones below:

- Reduces stress
- Reduces anxiety
- Helps prevent heart disease
- Lowers blood pressure
- Lowers heart rate
- Reduces chronic pain
- Improves sleep
- Alleviates gastrointestinal difficulties
- Reduces depression
- Reduces anxiety disorders
- Regulates emotions
- Improves self-control
- Helps overcome obsessive-compulsive disorder symptoms
- Helps in the treatment of substance abuse
- Helps in the treatment of self-harming
- Increases life satisfaction, wellbeing and happiness
- Helps you savour life's pleasures
- Helps you to become more engaged
- Helps you be in the present
- Reduces rumination
- Reduces worry over the future
- Enables you to have deep connection with others
- Creates more empathy for self and others
- Creates more gratitude
- Aids relaxation
- Enables you to be comfortable with yourself
- Enables you to listen to your inner self
- Enables you to know your inner self
- Enables you to be aware of others
- Develops parts of the brain related to happiness, decision-making and self-regulation
- Protects from the effects of cortisol, the stress hormone

CHAPTER **3**

Positivity

Barbara Fredrickson, a Positive Psychologist based in North Carolina, has done years of research on positivity and developed what she calls the Broaden and Build theory. She believes that when the mind is in a positive state it is more open, receptive and flexible – hence the term "broaden". This broadening can happen in the short term and help things in the moment, but it is also beneficial in the long term. The long-term benefits of feeling positive on a regular basis are that we build our "resources".

These resources are:

- **Psychological** – for example, resilience and optimism

- **Physical** – for example, cardiovascular health

- **Intellectual** – for example, the ability to absorb information

- **Social** – for example, the ability to make new connections and strengthen existing relationships

The great thing is that each resource fuels itself, so as you become more positive you benefit more and more, your mind broadens and your resources build all the time – it's a wonderful upward spiral.

THE NEGATIVITY BIAS

However, we need to be aware of negativity. A negativity bias can be found within us all, as it is in fact a survival instinct. Our brains are more attuned to negative things rather than positive or neutral things, in order to keep us out of danger. If we miss something negative in our environment, such as a person or beast running toward us in an aggressive manner, it could potentially kill us. Whereas missing something positive or neutral is unlikely to cause us any harm.

Furthermore, when our brains go into a negative state they narrow in focus. This makes perfect sense on an evolutionary level, as when danger is approaching, we need to be able to focus all our attention on it and shut out everything else that is irrelevant, so that we can react quickly and effectively.

This changing of focus is a great skill that has no doubt played a large part in the survival of the species. However, if we do not switch out of this negative thinking after a situation has occurred, then we can get locked into thinking negatively all the time. When our minds are locked into a narrow focus, it makes all the benefits of broadening and building difficult or impossible. Our minds become rigid, narrow, fixed and closed. This is an unhealthy state of mind and one that results in problematic relationships, to say the very least.

Ideally, we need to consciously shift our awareness into a positive state. To do this, we need to acknowledge that our minds will often draw our attention more strongly toward the negative, so we need to mindfully refocus and retrain our brains into being aware of all the positives around us and shift into a positive mindset.

This does not mean that you will stop being aware of the negatives, or any potential dangers – you are hardwired to notice those and always will. However, it does mean you will gain a better balance, have a more realistic view of the world and have expanded awareness in general.

Shining a Light on Positivity

When the mind is in a positive state, imagine that it is like a wide beam of light lighting up a vast area. The mind in a negative state, however, could be compared to a narrow spotlight, focused only on the one thing that it perceives as negative or dangerous.

The Power of Laughter

Laughter makes us more positive. It is also a powerful way of helping us change our perspective and allowing us to cope better.

When the effects of negativity set in – for example, if we are stressed about a work situation – our way of seeing things becomes narrow and rigid. However, if we can laugh or make a joke about it our minds will broaden and our creativity will begin to expand as we become more positive. We will then be able to think of different ways to handle the situation.

According to Rod Martin, Professor of Psychology at the University of Western Ontario, there are four styles of humour. These are:

- **Self-enhancing** – this is the ability to laugh at life, make a joke when something unfortunate happens, laughing at yourself in a good-natured way. It is difficult to be anxious, angry or stressed if you are genuinely laughing at something. This kind of humour carries a feeling of self-acceptance and tolerance toward yourself and others.

- **Affiliative** – this is inclusive, relatable humour – for example, witty banter and telling jokes. This kind of humour helps us create better relationships, as well as helping us all cope with whatever comes our way in life.

- **Aggressive** – this is teasing, sarcasm and ridicule. It excludes and rejects people and can be used to manipulate or criticize. Therefore, it tends to erode relationships over time.

- **Self-defeating** – this is when we make fun of ourselves to others. It carries underlying hostility and lack of tolerance toward ourselves.

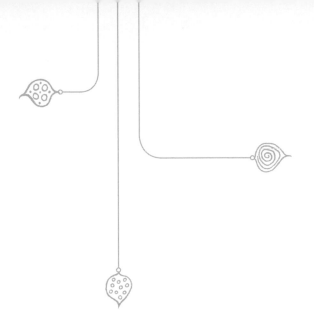

Generally speaking, the first two are positive while the last two are negative – although whether humour is received as positive or negative depends on the context and timing.

When I was a child, my dyslexia and dyspraxia used to cause me stress. They were undiagnosed, so nobody, including myself, understood or knew what was happening, which caused me anxiety. As an adult, I often laugh at the things I do or say that are a result of my dyslexia or dyspraxia – it is a good source of entertainment for me. However, I am not laughing at myself in a self-defeating way.

Try It Out:
Laugh and Change

There are many ways to use humour to change your perspective and increase your enjoyment of life. Here are some examples for you to try:

- **Laugh at yourself** – we often take ourselves or life too seriously. Being able to laugh at yourself is a great way to lighten up inside.

- **Make a joke out of a difficult situation** – obviously, it's important to be sensitive to the situation, but it's a great coping mechanism. My brother and son have always been great at making me laugh by making a kind joke out of my situation, particularly when life is tough. They assure me they are laughing with me and not at me!

- **Use visible reminders** – if you find it hard to lighten up, give yourself a visible reminder by putting an object on your desk, or a picture on the fridge. At the very least you will smile, but hopefully you will laugh too.

- **Share funny stories** – making another person or a group of people laugh is as pleasurable as someone making you laugh, and it can bring you closer together.

- **Seek out playful, funny friends** – we are generally subconsciously drawn to these people anyway.

- **Allow your inner child to come out** – be silly, have fun with your partner, friends and family, and play with your children.

- **Try to laugh every day** – if you can't laugh one day, then try to make up for it the following day.

- **Smile!** – the very act of smiling makes us feel better. Even if we force and hold a smile for two minutes, it will make us feel better.

Smiles All Around

- Research has shown that participants even feel happier when they are unable to frown after having Botox. And, conversely, they were not as happy when they were given Botox to suppress the facial muscles involved in smiling.

- According to research (conducted by Hewlett Packard), one smile can result in the same pleasure as 2,000 bars of chocolate.

- There is a big difference between how many times per day an adult smiles and a child smiles. It is thought that kids smile up to 20 times more than adults.

- Smiling is a very important form of communication – it is one of the few universal means of communicating. Another wonderful thing about smiling is that it is contagious – so pass it on.

The Power of Three

Studies have shown for every negative comment or incident, we need to balance it out with at least three positive comments. This can be obvious in relationships of whatever type, whether they're romantic or professional, or with friends, family or neighbours. If the balance of positive/negative comments goes lower than 3:1 then it begins to have a bad effect on the relationship and the people within that relationship. If that happens on a regular basis, then the relationship will most likely break down or have some sort of crisis. However, if the balance is above 3:1, then the relationship will be positive and fulfilling.

Another benefit to a good balance is that tolerance will build up within the relationship. This is like subconsciously saving up the positivity for a rainy day. All the extra positives are saved up, so if the relationship has a difficult patch (which most relationships do), then the positives in the bank will result in those involved being more tolerant of each other during that time. Therefore, they deal with the difficulties in a more constructive way and may be able to strengthen and grow their relationship as a result.

When problems are dealt with in that manner, it gives everyone involved confidence in each other's ability to resolve things, knowing the relationship is strong enough to cope with any issues.

Positive on the Inside

We need to be aware of the positivity within ourselves too. Spend the day noticing how you talk to yourself, and what your inner dialogue is like. You can then estimate how many times you speak to yourself positively compared to negatively.

It is common for us to be positive toward other people, yet be harsh and negative toward ourselves. Once you become aware of your inner dialogue, you can ask yourself if you would say that to a friend – you'll find the answer is usually "No".

It's amazing how we find it acceptable to be so harsh, judgemental and sometimes just plain nasty toward ourselves. It's really important to work on shifting this inner dialogue to a more positive, supportive and understanding voice. This will be discussed further in the Relationships chapter (see page 178).

Acknowledging Negative Emotions

Being positive does not mean you are not allowed to have negative emotions. In fact, it would be harmful if you repressed or denied negative feelings, especially if they were appropriate for the situation. For example, if a loved one dies then it is natural to be upset – it would not be healthy to deny or try to suppress those feelings. We must allow ourselves to feel whatever emotions arise, to acknowledge them, to understand the origins of them, to express them and then decide on the best way to address them.

The fact is there are no positive or negative emotions, as such – all emotions are good emotions. The words "negative" and "positive" are used to explain theories and processes. So, for most of us, perhaps better terms would be "appropriate" and "inappropriate" emotions, or "beneficial" and "harmful" emotions.

The skill is knowing yourself well enough to know what the most beneficial response would be for you in each moment – that's not easy but it does come over time and it is definitely helped by mindfulness meditation (see page 66). A lot of people go to the doctor saying they are depressed, for example, and antidepressants are prescribed sometimes without understanding, or addressing, what is causing that feeling of depression.

Antidepressants might mask the feeling but they won't solve whatever is causing the feeling of depression – it is always important to understand and acknowledge what you are feeling. It might be due to relationship difficulties, family problems, financial problems, work-related problems and so on.

Mindfulness meditation helps us become aware of what we are really feeling, to see the roots of those feelings and to allow us to express and release them. Simply put, it is about being authentic to yourself first, and then to others if you can.

"*Without rain, nothing grows. Learn to embrace the storms of your life.*"

Invoking Positivity Every Day

When we look at photos, it evokes different emotions within us. You can look at a photo of a loved one, for example, and feel love that dissolves any negative emotions you may be feeling. Or you can look at a photo of a funny moment which will always make you laugh, a beautiful place that makes you feel awe or a pet that makes you smile – the list is endless. But the point is, in a very short amount of time, you can shift your mindset and not only feel happier within yourself but also experience the benefits of a positive mindset.

If you are waiting to go into a job interview and are feeling nervous, a quick glance at a great photo on your phone can really help. It will shift the anxiety (which is going to narrow your mind and make you perform less ably at the interview) to a positive feeling so that you can be the best version of yourself.

In fact, it will always help to be in a positive mindset in any situation in which you need to be able to connect with people, to be intellectually sharper, more creative or more resilient. So enjoy creating a positivity album of a set of pictures that shift your mindset.

POSITIVITY THROUGH MUSIC

Music has multiple benefits. It is very evocative, so a song or a piece of music can create a strong emotion, depending on your association with it. Listen to music that evokes positive, happy feelings within you. Have fun choosing and creating a positivity playlist that you can use to get into a positive mindset whenever you choose.

Dopamine – a mood-enhancing, pleasure chemical – is released into our brains when we experience pleasure (including when we have an orgasm) and research shows we can have two dopamine hits while listening to music. The first hit can come when you hear the first few bars and realize it is a song you really love. The next dopamine release comes while you are actually listening to the song.

If you like dancing, then you can add an extra boost of positivity by dancing along. And singing along will also boost feel-good dopamine levels – don't worry whether you can sing or not, just enjoy it!

Try It Out:
A Positivity Playlist

Listening to music is a fantastic way to feel positive in a matter of minutes. Make a playlist of some of your favourite songs on your phone, so it is always with you. Notice how you feel before and after you play any music.

THE POWER OF COMEDY

Video clips (on sites such as YouTube) are another great way to instantly and easily make you laugh, whatever your sense of humour. You can watch these during your lunch hour, particularly if your work is stressful, to help you relax and reset. If you are going to a difficult meeting you are anxious about, watching a couple of YouTube videos will help you be in a better mental state to deal more effectively with the situation.

Similarly, if you end a stressful day by watching a comedy show on TV or online, then that too will reduce your stress level. Remember that humour does you good in many ways – it lowers stress, aids your memory, releases endorphins (the feel-good chemical) and helps you maintain a healthy heart too.

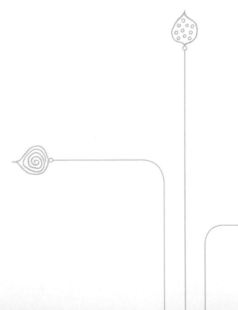

The Top Benefits of Positivity

With more positivity in your life, you will enjoy:
- Greater resilience
- More optimism
- The ability to make new social connections and improve existing relationships
- More open-mindedness and flexibility
- The ability to absorb information more easily
- Greater creativity
- Greater life satisfaction
- A more positive perception of the world
- A greater ability to overcome negative emotions
- Physical benefits, such as improved cardiovascular health
- Better sleep
- Greater feelings of happiness

CHAPTER 4

Resilience

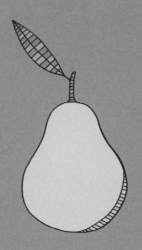

Resilience is the ability to adapt positively to significant risk, adversity, trauma, threat, tragedy or a high-stress situation. However, it does not mean we will not suffer or feel emotional distress – this would be unnatural. Resilience is about having a natural emotional response and then, in due course, bouncing back.

How long it takes to overcome and recover depends on the situation, the individual and the circumstances. There is no right or wrong – the more you can let go of any judgement on yourself, or others, the better. Judgement will only add to the stress of the situation and hinder the recovery process. Ideally, you will be open and non-judgemental to whatever emotions arise, letting them out and not trying to suppress them. Be compassionate toward yourself, as well as others (this will be discussed further in the chapter on Relationships, see page 178).

As discussed in the introduction on page 17, research shows that we often overestimate the effects that situations cause and underestimate how quickly we are able to adapt to new situations. Resilience is the ability to bounce back to the same level of happiness or life satisfaction as before the traumatic event. We also have the ability to bounce up to a higher level of happiness. This is known as Post Traumatic Growth (PTG), which I will discuss later in the chapter.

What Makes Us Resilient?

Resilience can be learned and developed over time. Various pieces of research have shown there are many factors, both external and internal, that help us with resilience. These include:

EXTERNAL FACTORS

- Environment
- Family
- Social circle
- Belief system
- Ability to ask for help
- Resilient role models

INTERNAL FACTORS

- Personal wellbeing
- Self-esteem
- Belief system, spirituality, faith
- Ability to perceive bad times as temporary
- Belief in ourselves
- Ability to recognize our strengths (see page 132)
- Hope and belief the future will be better than the present (see page 142)
- Positivity (see page 86)
- Creativity and problem-solving skills (see page 126)
- Grit and self-regulation (see page 175)
- Our meaning and motivation (see page 162)
- Maintaining positive inner dialogue (see page 95)
- Self-compassion (see page 182)
- Autonomy

Having a past experience of resilience also builds one's confidence – knowing you have been through difficult times before means you know you can do it again.

Respond Actively

It is important to have an active response to trauma. An active response will mean you feel empowered, while a passive response is disempowering and means you are more likely to feel like a victim. If you can remain proactive, you will have a sense of control.

How you view adversity can change your experience of the situation and your ability to be resilient. It's best to avoid what is known as a "pessimistic explanatory style", where a person has a fixed view on a situation. Somebody who adopts this style often doesn't realize that several different viewpoints can be taken. The more rigidly a person views a situation, the more set they become in their position, which can lock them into a negative state. This state will then become entrenched over time, making it more difficult to escape from.

Watch Out

Watch out for black-and-white thinking that is good/bad or right/wrong, for example. Or (if you can) at the very least try to soften the edges. Everything changes, nothing is permanent – this truth is reassuring when we are going through bad times, but also when we are depressed or steeped in negativity, and it feels as though nothing will ever change and will always be this way. This is the nature of that particular mental state.

By trying to take a mindful observer's perspective (see exercise on page 119), you will be more able to see the situation for what it is, and therefore take steps to break free of it. Notice whether you think and talk in absolute, permanent or global terms, using words such as "always", "never" or "everyone". These often indicate that a person has a negative or depressed mindset.

Try to step back and gently ask yourself if it really is "always" or "never", for example. Your feelings are likely to answer "Yes", but if you look at the facts and evidence, you will often discover the reality is not "always" or "never".

There are, of course, exceptions but usually you come to realize that although the situation feels extreme or absolute, in reality it is not. That is how to start softening those hard edges and letting some light in. Slowly over time, and with effort, you can then work on increasing this attitude.

An optimistic explanatory style interprets difficulties and adversity as temporary, recognizing that things will change. It helps us see the bigger picture. We so often forget to stand back far enough to put things into their true perspective, to work out whether it matters as much as it might seem in the moment. An optimistic explanatory style can also be pinned down to specific causes, such as: "I didn't study enough to pass the exam", rather than the more general, "I'm rubbish and will never be able to pass this exam".

An optimistic style will result in resilience and a growth mindset (see page 30) and will approach difficulties as challenges to overcome. Meanwhile, the pessimistic style often results in helplessness, disempowerment and giving up. The research shows that an optimistic style leads to higher grades, improved athletic performance and even an improvement in how well a person recovers from heart-bypass surgery.

Resilience and Planning

Resilient people are more likely to plan for future events. This was demonstrated with the work of American developmental psychologist Dr Emmy Werner in Hawaii, where she researched resilience at the time of Hurricane Iniki in 1992. She observed that resilient people prepared better for the hurricane (by boarding up their windows and barricading their doors, for example), therefore reporting less damage.

Where are You?

Positive Psychology does not deny that difficulties happen or that life is hard at times. A common misperception is that Positive Psychology says "Just think positive" in response to adversity. This is not the case. Positive Psychology offers different interventions, techniques and coping strategies but, as discussed in the introduction (see page 23), it depends where you are within yourself as to whether Positive Psychology or regular psychology techniques will help.

However, wherever you are within yourself, I believe it is helpful to understand how the mind works in both a positive and negative state. That way you can better understand yourself and others, and then take appropriate action.

The key is how we respond to stress and difficulties, and a positive attitude will naturally help us deal with things better. Resilience is built through difficult times, and how we process, respond and act can have a large impact on our mental health and life as a whole. Let your trauma be what inspires or propels you and gives you meaning and motivation.

The main thing is to move forward and not worry about the speed you take – we all know the story of the hare and the tortoise. Try to develop self-awareness without harsh judgement, as this thinking stops us from being able to enjoy challenges. For example, babies repeat things over and over until they finally learn how to do them. There is no judgement, only pleasure (for them and for those watching) when they finally manage to walk,

.

Harsh judgement can make us feel embarrassed or ashamed by our mistakes – and embarrassment and shame are such uncomfortable feelings that we try to avoid mistakes in order to avoid the emotions. If we can think in terms of "try, fail, learn, try again" (in the way babies do), then we can have the chance to enjoy the challenge, and not worry about how many times we try, fail, learn and try again.

Positively You

It's important to make sure your inner dialogue is supportive, understanding and encouraging. As discussed in the Positivity chapter (see page 86), it is crucial to develop a positive inner voice. Make sure you commend yourself when you achieve something, no matter how small, and try to do this in the same way you would congratulate a friend. It can be astonishing how easily we minimize our own achievements.

Be careful not to ruminate, going over and over the same things in your mind while arriving at no particular conclusion. Rumination increases levels of the stress hormone cortisol, and is liable to take you into a deeper hole of depression or anxiety. This is another point where the skills developed within mindfulness meditation (see page 66) will help. During meditation you will learn how to redirect the mind to focus on the breath or the present moment, for example. Ideally you will develop this ability when life is good, so when life is difficult, you will have the tools ready to redirect the mind on to something more productive or, at least, less destructive.

Post Traumatic Growth

As mentioned earlier, resilience is the ability to bounce back to the same state of wellbeing as before the adversity. However, Post Traumatic Growth (PTG) is bouncing up to an even higher level than before the trauma. Giving meaning to an event will encourage PTG, and is also an effective coping strategy for traumatic events.

> *"Change is inevitable, growth is optional."*
>
> JOHN C. MAXWELL

Event

Before   After   RESILIENCE:
                    Same level before
Depressed   and after event

Event

After   PTG: Bounce up
         to higher level
Before   after event
Depressed

There are countless stories of people who have demonstrated resilience during difficult times. J.K. Rowling offers a wonderful example of resilience and PTG. Six months after the death of her mother, she began writing *Harry Potter*, all while she was a single mother, unemployed and on social security benefits. She was suffering from depression, was sometimes suicidal and sought therapeutic help. She wrote her book in a local café, often with her daughter in a pram next to her and, when she finally finished it, it was rejected by many publishers. She is now one of the UK's best-selling living authors and one of the richest women in the world.

Take the PTG Test

Take this test to indicate the degree of change that has occurred as a result of the crisis/disaster you experienced. Below are some statements about your experiences. Note down how you feel about the statements, according to the following scale:

SCORE:

0 – *I did not experience this change as a result of my crisis*
1 – *I experienced this change to a very small degree as a result of my crisis*
2 – *I experienced this change to a small degree as a result of my crisis*
3 – *I experienced this change to a moderate degree as a result of my crisis*
4 – *I experienced this change to a great degree as a result of my crisis*
5 – *I experienced this change to a very great degree as a result of my crisis*

POSSIBLE AREAS OF GROWTH AND CHANGE:

1 I changed my priorities about what is important in life
2 I have a greater appreciation for the value of my own life
3 I developed new interests
4 I have a greater feeling of self-reliance
5 I have a better understanding of spiritual matters
6 I more clearly see that I can count on people in times of trouble
7 I established a new path for my life
8 I have a greater sense of closeness with others
9 I am more willing to express my emotions
10 I know better that I can handle difficulties
11 I am able to do better things with my life
12 I am better able to accept the way things work out
13 I can better appreciate each day
14 New opportunities are available, which wouldn't have been otherwise
15 I have more compassion for others
16 I put more effort into my relationships
17 I am more likely to try to change things that need changing
18 I have a stronger spiritual belief
19 I discovered that I'm stronger than I thought I was
20 I learned a great deal about how wonderful people are
21 I better accept needing others

Now add up all the scores and read on to discover how to interpret your score.

Interpreting Your Score on the PTG Test

Whatever your score is, please take time to reflect on all that you have been through, what you have had to overcome and what you are still struggling to overcome. Think about what you would say to your best friend if they had been through the same and say that to yourself. Apply that compassion to yourself as you acknowledge and commend yourself for all you have achieved – no matter where you are in terms of PTG. PTG will come if you are compassionate and supportive of yourself – it is only a matter of time.

Between 0 and 21
Very low

Recovering from trauma is extremely difficult and takes time. Practise self-compassion to help you cope with your trauma, be gentle and kind to yourself. Sometimes just surviving is a massive accomplishment in itself – the PTG will come in due course.

Between 22 and 42
Low

You have achieved some PTG, which is fantastic. Commend yourself for what you have accomplished, recognize what you have been through and what it has taken to get to where you are right now. When you are ready, you could continue to build on the upward trajectory you have started.

Between 43 and 63
Medium

The PTG is happening, and you are doing really well. Life is likely to be feeling a bit easier now, as your PTG is picking up momentum. Make sure you continue to take care of yourself to ensure you stay on track, moving in the right direction.

Between 64 and 84
High

PTG is being felt across the board – it might be helpful to see how you score in each category (see page 114) to understand where you are flourishing. Take time to reflect on all that you have achieved, and fully acknowledge and commend yourself for it.

Between 85 and 105
Very high

Wow, what you have achieved is amazing! Your life has fundamentally changed since your trauma, in nearly, if not all, ways. You should be proud of yourself and all you have done. You are an inspiration to yourself and those who know you.

INDIVIDUAL CATEGORIES WITHIN THE PTG TEST

The statements within the test also fall into separate categories. Total your scores within each category to give yourself a deeper understanding of where you are in each (the more we understand about ourselves and our situation, the more we can address the situation in the way we feel is most appropriate.).

Category 1: Relating to Others
Total your scores for questions 6, 8, 9, 15, 16, 20 and 21.

Between 0 and 8 – Low
Between 9 and 17 – Medium
Between 18 and 26 – High
Between 27 and 35 – Very high

Category 2: New Possibilities
Total your scores for questions 3, 7, 11, 14 and 17.

Between 0 and 5 – Low
Between 6 and 12 – Medium
Between 13 and 19 – High
Between 20 and 25 – Very high

Category 3: Personal Strengths
Total your scores for questions 4, 10, 12 and 19.

Between 0 and 4 – Low
Between 5 and 10 – Medium
Between 11 and 16 – High
Between 17 and 20 – Very high

Category 4: Spiritual Change
Total your scores for questions 5 and 18.

Between 0 and 2 – Low
Between 3 and 5 – Medium
Between 6 and 8 – High
Between 9 and 10 – Very high

Category 5: Appreciation of Life
Total your scores for questions 1, 2 and 13.

Between 0 and 3 – Low
Between 4 and 7 – Medium
Between 8 and 11 – High
Between 12 and 15 – Very high

PTG RESEARCH

There has been research into PTG covering a whole range of traumas, such as bereavement, natural disasters, terrorist attacks, chronic illness, cancer and much more. It doesn't matter what type of trauma a person has experienced, there are certain factors that are recognized as being key to PTG. In fact, most of the aspects discussed in this book are associated with PTG. Perhaps by this stage you may be able to guess that they are:

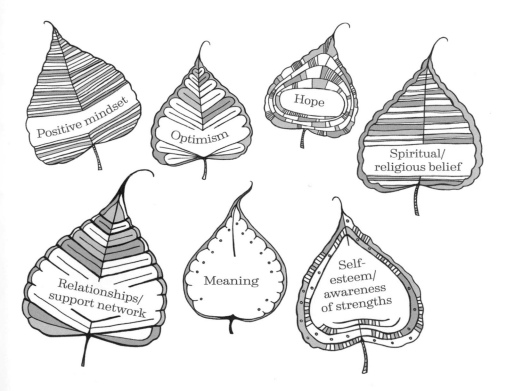

Positive mindset

Optimism

Hope

Spiritual/ religious belief

Relationships/ support network

Meaning

Self-esteem/ awareness of strengths

Giving yourself time to process and think through the trauma is important. This gives you the ability to start to come to a level of acceptance and to reinterpret what has happened in a positive light. Positive reinterpretation is learning to focus on the positive within a situation and finding meaning in what happened. This can take time but is a key factor to being able to achieve PTG.

Case Study:
Thinking Again

My father died very unexpectedly while I was abroad on holiday. It soon transpired that the cause of death was down to "mistakes" by the doctor and hospital in the treatment of a relatively simple illness. Naturally, I was plunged into shock and deep mourning. However, the positive reinterpretation that I eventually came to was that my father died when he was still working full time, playing tennis several times a week and still vibrant. I knew he would have hated to, in his own words, "become an old man". He wouldn't have wanted to be unable to do all the things he loved – he was not someone who would have aged gracefully. I worked through my emotions and was able to come to a place of acceptance, realize a positive reinterpretation of what had happened and attribute a meaning to it, therefore eventually achieving PTG.

SIGNS OF CHANGE

Research shows that, over time, PTG will ideally be experienced in the five following areas:

1. Relationships with others

2. New possibilities in life

3. Personal strength

4. Spiritual change

5. Appreciation of life/gratitude

Research highlights how PTG reduces distress and helps people positively adjust. They feel stronger as they realize the strengths and abilities they were previously unaware of – this positively changes how they view themselves. Their relationships are strengthened and deepened, due to the support they receive and give. They are able to become more compassionate toward themselves and others. Hope increases as their goals change and they see new possibilities in life. They also report changes in their life philosophy, priorities and spirituality.

THE WAY TO NAVIGATE

It is not the type of event that dictates a person's ability to achieve PTG, but the way they process it after the trauma. Denial and avoidance only serve to prolong pain, especially if some sort of substance (whether that's food, drink or drugs) is used to enhance the denial and avoidance.

Watch Out

Watch out not to put pressure on yourself to be positive or attribute meaning until you have gone through the natural emotion following the difficulty you experienced. It takes time to work through painful emotions and to get to a place where you are ready to open up to the Positive Psychology I am discussing.

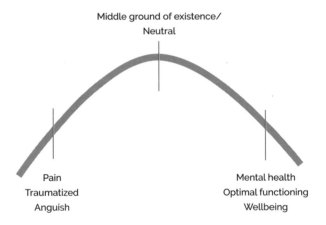

Middle ground of existence/
Neutral

Pain
Traumatized
Anguish

Mental health
Optimal functioning
Wellbeing

Ideally you might use mainstream psychology to help you get from a place of deep pain and anguish to a neutral place. From here, Positive Psychology techniques can be introduced. Remember it can be difficult to navigate our emotions, especially after trauma, so professional help can guide you through and out the other side.

Try it Out:
Mindful Observer's Perspective

The point of the following exercise is to try to detach, or at least step back, from negative or unhelpful emotions. Emotions can consume us and, when they do, it is difficult, if not impossible, to think clearly. Hence, we are prone to saying and doing things that we later regret.

The moment you are aware of the emotion, label it. Often when we are consumed by an emotion, such as anger, our focus shifts on to the person we are angry with and we are not mindful of what is going on within ourselves. If you are having an argument, you might midway through realize how angry you are. When this happens, change how you label the emotion – try thinking "*There is* anger" rather than "*I am* angry". The latter is an easy mistake. When we say "I am angry", we identify with the anger and *our* ego attaches to it. This means we hold on to it even longer than we would do otherwise because it is our anger. But we need to do the opposite, we want to try to detach from it, unhook our ego and say "There is anger" like an interested and curious observer.

The moment you become mindful of the emotion and label it "There is..." the intensity of the emotion will start to decrease. You adopt the interested, curious observer's perspective who says "That is interesting, look at that emotion".

Once you have noticed the emotion, try to remove yourself from the situation for a few minutes. Try going outside or into a quiet room. Notice where in your body you feel the effect of that emotion – is it in the stomach or chest? Can you feel tension in the muscles? In the shoulders or jaw? How is your breathing? Is it shallow and fast?

Watch Out

Beware of the ego as it might try to hold on to the emotion, justifying it by identifying with it. In other words, watch out for thoughts that contain "I", "me" or "my". For example, you might say: "Yes, but that was *my* car." For now let it go, now is a time to get the forest fire under control. Once the emotion has lessened you can resume your mindful living – that is intelligent, conscious and compassionate thought, action and speech.

Putting Out Fires

Emotions are like forest fires – once they catch they can spread really quickly, making them difficult to control and put out. Ideally you will notice that initial spark of emotion and, just like a spark in the forest, if seen early enough, it will be easy to extinguish.

The more you develop in meditation, and therefore mindfulness, the more you will feel whatever emotion arises, and make the choice to allow it to grow or put it out – whatever is the most beneficial thing to do. Again, it is about being able to make that conscious choice, to be aware of the choice you are making and why you are doing it.

It takes time and practice to feel emotions at the initial stage. To start with, try labelling your emotions as soon as you become aware of them, even if they have already reached "forest fire" level. Don't worry what stage the emotion is at, just be pleased that you became mindful of it. The more you practise, the earlier you will notice them arising. Also, the more you commend yourself (rather than berate yourself), you will naturally start to notice the emotions earlier.

Watch Out
Watch out for judging the emotions that arise – be aware of judgements and let them go. Being non-judgemental is an important aspect of mindfulness. Also, be careful not to judge yourself for judging. If you can see it as human nature then it's easier to smile at it and let it go.

The Top Benefits of Resilience

More resilience in your life will:
- Help you positively adapt to adversity
- Build confidence
- Make you better prepared for future events
- Improve your relationships
- Enable Post-Traumatic Growth. which in turn:
  - Strengthens and deepens relationships
  - Opens new possibilities in life
  - Improves personal strength
  - Leads to greater spirituality
  - Positively changes life philosophy
  - Positively changes priorities
  - Improves appreciation for life
  - Reduces distress
  - Increases compassion to self and others
  - Increases hope

CHAPTER **5**

Awareness
of Strengths

Being aware of our strengths and making use of them on a regular basis has a lasting effect on our happiness and wellbeing. However, according to research conducted in the UK in 2001, two-thirds of participants did not know what their strengths were when asked. So it stands to reason that if we don't know what our strengths are, then we don't know whether we are using them or not.

Research conducted by Gallup showed that the more people use their strengths, the better they feel. In fact, not only do they report feeling happier, but they also feel more energetic and smile and laugh more. Feelings of anger, stress and worry are also significantly decreased.

How Do I Know My Strengths?

There are several different tests you can do to discover your strengths, but the one I always recommend is the Values In Action (VIA) Classification of Character Strengths. It is easy to do online and I prefer it because it is reliable, valid and well researched, with contributions from top academics in the field. It is also suitable for people in different countries and cultures, not just the Western world. And, finally, the focus is on character strengths and core virtues, which are valued in their own right, as opposed to talents, which are valued for their tangible consequences.

1. Wisdom and Knowledge

The people who created VIA Character Strengths reviewed classic texts from Buddhism, Taoism, Confucius, Ancient Greece, Judeo-Christianity, Islam and Hinduism, to create the six overarching virtues. These virtues stand up to cross-cultural research done in 75 different countries. They are:

4. Justice

2. Courage

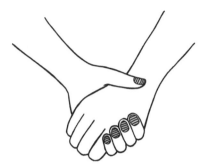

3. Humanity

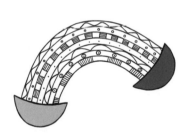

5. Temperance

6. Transcendence

These six virtues are then broken down further to show the various ways the virtues can be expressed. For example, Courage can be demonstrated through bravery, perseverance, honesty and vitality. The list on the following pages has all the overarching virtues and the character strengths within them.

The VIA Classification of Character Strengths

 1. Wisdom and Knowledge

These cognitive strengths entail the acquisition and use of knowledge.

- *Creativity* (originality, ingenuity): Thinking of novel and productive ways to conceptualize and do things; includes artistic achievement but is not limited to it.
- *Curiosity* (interest, novelty-seeking, openness to experience): Taking an interest in ongoing experience for its own sake; finding subjects and topics fascinating; exploring and discovering.
- *Judgement* (critical thinking): Thinking things through and examining them from all sides; not jumping to conclusions; being able to change one's mind in light of evidence; weighing all evidence fairly.
- *Love of learning:* Mastering new skills, topics and bodies of knowledge, whether on one's own or formally; obviously related to the strength of curiosity but goes beyond it to describe the tendency to add systematically to what one knows.
- *Perspective* (wisdom): Being able to provide wise counsel to others; having ways of looking at the world that make sense to oneself and to other people.

 2. Courage

These emotional strengths involve the exercise of will to accomplish goals in the face of opposition, external or internal.

- *Bravery* (valour): Not shrinking from threat, challenge, difficulty or pain; speaking up for what is right even if there is opposition; acting on convictions even if unpopular; includes physical bravery but is not limited to it.
- *Perseverance* (persistence, industriousness): Finishing what one starts; persisting in a course of action in spite of obstacles; "getting it out the door"; taking pleasure in completing tasks.
- *Honesty* (authenticity, integrity): Speaking the truth but more broadly presenting oneself in a genuine way and acting in a sincere way; being without pretence; taking responsibility for one's feelings and actions.
- *Zest* (vitality, enthusiasm, vigour, energy): Approaching life with excitement and energy; not doing things halfway or half-heartedly; living life as an adventure; feeling alive and activated.

3. Humanity

These interpersonal strengths involve tending and befriending others.

- *Love:* Valuing close relations with others, in particular those in which sharing and caring are reciprocated; being close to other people.
- *Kindness* (generosity, nurturance, care, compassion, altruistic love, "niceness"): Doing favours and good deeds for others; helping them; taking care of them.
- *Social intelligence* (emotional intelligence, personal intelligence): Being aware of the motives and feelings of other people and oneself; knowing what to do to fit into different social situations; knowing what makes other people tick.

4. Justice

These civic strengths underlie healthy community life.

- *Teamwork* (citizenship, social responsibility, loyalty): Working well as a member of a group or team; being loyal to the group; doing one's share.
- *Fairness:* Treating all people the same according to notions of fairness and justice; not letting personal feelings bias decisions about others; giving everyone a fair chance.
- *Leadership:* Encouraging a group of which one is a member to get things done and at the same time maintain good relations within the group; organizing group activities and seeing that they happen.

5. Temperance

These strengths protect against excess.

- *Forgiveness:* Forgiving those who have done wrong; accepting the shortcomings of others; giving people a second chance; not being vengeful.

- *Humility:* Letting one's accomplishments speak for themselves; not regarding oneself as more special than one is.

- *Prudence:* Being careful about one's choices; not taking undue risks; not saying or doing things that might later be regretted.

- *Self-regulation* (self-control): Regulating what one feels and does; being disciplined; controlling one's appetites and emotions.

6. Transcendence

These strengths forge connections to the larger universe and provide meaning.

- *Appreciation of beauty and excellence* (awe, wonder, elevation): Noticing and appreciating beauty, excellence, and/or skilled performance in various domains of life, from nature to art to mathematics to science to everyday experience.

- *Gratitude:* Being aware of and thankful for the good things that happen; taking time to express thanks.

- *Hope* (optimism, future-mindedness, future orientation): Expecting the best in the future and working to achieve it; believing that a good future is something that can be brought about.

- *Humour* (playfulness): Liking to laugh and tease; bringing smiles to other people; seeing the light side; making (not necessarily telling) jokes.

- *Spirituality* (faith, purpose): Having coherent beliefs about the higher purpose and meaning of the universe; knowing where one fits within the larger scheme; having beliefs about the meaning of life that shape conduct and provide comfort.

Developing a Strengths Vocabulary

As mental health has been studied for many years, people have a greater vocabulary for describing mental health issues, whereas the vocabulary for describing strengths can often be limited. VIA provides a common vocabulary which helps people recognize and acknowledge those strengths within themselves, as well as others.

The two creators of the VIA Classification of Strengths, Christopher Peterson and Martin Seligman, were looking to create a catalogue of character strengths as a counterbalance to the Diagnostic and Statistical Manual of Mental Disorders (DSM), which is a catalogue of mental disorders. Like the DSM, VIA will also evolve and grow over time as understanding changes and develops.

Do You Know Your Strengths?

It is interesting to compare the results of the VIA survey with what you think your strengths are before you take the survey. So, before you do the VIA survey, write down:

• Five of your weaknesses

• Five of your strengths

Did you find it easier to write your five weaknesses, compared to your strengths? Most people are able to quickly and easily list their weaknesses, but then struggle to list their strengths. This is because they often have difficulty in finding the words to describe their strengths, yet have no difficulty finding the words to describe their weaknesses. This shows that many of us must develop our vocabulary and understanding of strengths, and become comfortable talking about them, without feeling like we are being arrogant.

The other reason this happens is because of the negativity bias discussed in the Positivity chapter (see page 86) and, also, what is known as "strengths blindness". Strengths blindness is not appreciating our own strengths because we undermine them and dismiss them as "normal" or not as valuable as strengths we see in other people. We may recognize and appreciate strengths in others yet dismiss, undermine and undervalue our own strengths. Let me emphasize the point that *all* strengths are equal – they are *all* important and valuable. We want to live in a world where people have different strengths and those differences are appreciated. That is how we can live, work and love in harmony.

It is important that we appreciate our own strengths as much as other people's. So, be mindful of counteracting any strengths blindness that you may have, understanding what you are doing and working on, and actually appreciating your own strengths.

Try It Out:
Take the VIA survey

You can take the VIA survey at www.viacharacter.org. It is available in multiple languages and there is also a youth version for people aged 10–17. Once you know your top character strengths (the first six, for example), then you can have fun purposely and mindfully using them.

After you have taken the survey, consider the following:

• Are any of your top six strengths the same as the ones you wrote down before the survey?

• How often do you currently use each of your top strengths on a monthly, weekly or daily basis?

• Focusing on a single strength at a time, spend as much time as possible throughout the week using it. Try to find new and creative ways to use that strength.

• Note down how using each strength makes you feel.

• Which new practices do you particularly enjoy and how do they impact on your wellbeing and life satisfaction?

Signature Strengths

Awareness of your strengths can enable you to become the best version of yourself, helping you to be mindful of those strengths and make decisions based on them.

Our top strengths are also known as our "signature strengths" as they are unique to us. People may share the same strengths but what will differ is the balance and combination of those strengths. Also, how we combine and use different strengths to achieve our goals is unique to us. Signature strengths are core to our identity, they are usually how people who know us well would describe us. They will come naturally and easily and we will feel energized when we use them.

The more connected you are to your signature strengths, the more motivated, fulfilled and satisfied you will feel whatever you are doing. Businesses and recruitment teams are beginning to realize that character strengths are more important than what people do, as they result in greater satisfaction, engagement, motivation and meaning at work.

Similar results are found in relationships. The more partners appreciate each other's strengths, the better the relationship. Research shows greater satisfaction in a relationship results in more commitment, intimacy and support. This will be discussed in the Relationships chapter later in the book (see page 178).

Watch Out

The thing to watch out for when it comes to strengths is the underuse or overuse of them – balance is the key. Both underuse or overuse of our strengths can have consequences.

Underuse of strengths is easier to spot and understand – particularly because of the negativity bias, we are often drawn to focusing on our so called weaknesses. People sometimes focus on the strengths that come at the bottom of their list rather than their top strengths. However, it is worth thinking about how the underuse of those bottom strengths may affect you and those around you.

For example, let's take curiosity – it's great to take an interest in the things and people you encounter. However, we have all experienced meeting people who bombard us with questions, which feels like they are being nosy and interrogating us rather than just taking an interest. Similarly, there are people who show no interest at all and it can come across as arrogant and rude.

Another example is zest. In overuse, a person can come across as hyperactive and exhausting to be around. But with underuse, a person can be so sedentary that they appear lazy, lacking energy and enthusiasm, and are hard work to be with. Ideally, zest is about being vital, having energy and enthusiasm for life and all that you do, which makes you inspiring and enjoyable company.

Research indicates that social anxiety is associated with the overuse of social intelligence and humility, and the underuse of zest, humour and self-regulation.

Again, balance is the key here (hence it is a theme throughout the book). Naturally, you will be more inclined toward your signature strengths, less inclined toward the strengths at the end of the list, and somewhere in the middle for the others.

A Show of Strength

Imagine every strength as being on a scale, with one end being underuse, the other end being overuse, and the halfway point as optimal. Here are some examples:

◄— Underuse	STRENGTH	Overuse —►
Indifference	CURIOSITY	Intrusiveness
Inauthenticity	HONESTY	Virtuousness
Lethargy	ZEST	Hyperactivity
Apathy	LOVE	Idolatry
Unforgiving	FORGIVENESS	Overly forgiving
Unawareness	APPRECIATION OF BEAUTY	Perfectionism
Immorality	SPIRITUALITY	Extremism
Over-seriousness	HUMOUR	Foolishness

Case Study:
It Takes Two

I had a client whose top strength was gratitude. She had a grateful outlook on life, but the negative impact of its overuse was seen in her relationship. She had an unhealthy, unbalanced relationship where she gave and her partner took, and it seldom went the other way. Her partner made little effort in their relationship and contributed very little on an emotional or physical level.

He did not celebrate her successes nor support her during her difficulties, as she did for him. He did not plan or organize any outings or things for them to do, and showed no appreciation toward her when she did these things throughout their relationship.

Her overuse of gratitude meant she focused on the things she was grateful for, which enabled her to let go of the things that bothered her. She struggled to stand back enough to look at the big picture and see the relationship as a whole. Over time this resulted in the erosion of her self-worth and self-esteem and she was more and more unhappy in the relationship.

Inevitably, there came a point where the relationship was so unbalanced that she saw the reality of the situation and was able to walk away.

Interestingly, research shows that a tendency toward forgiveness leads to continued psychological and physical aggression in relationships. This is another example of the importance of self-worth and self-compassion – respecting and taking care of oneself enough to take the appropriate action.

AM I OVERDOING IT?

It is not always easy to recognize when we are overusing our strengths – a lot of introspection and self-awareness are needed (both of which develop naturally when we practise meditation and mindfulness, see page 66).

If you are at the starting point of learning about your strengths, then focus on discovering what your strengths are and using them on a regular basis. Don't worry about overuse or underuse at this point, let that come later.

If you are already aware of your strengths, what you wrote before the survey matched your top six VIA strengths and you are using those strengths on a regular basis, then move on to developing your awareness of underuse and overuse. Refine and find that lovely balance point.

It's interesting to note that people who gain success based on their talents, but not connected to their character strengths, often report feeling successful but have a lack of satisfaction.

Try It Out:
Ask Yourself

Ask yourself the following questions:

- How have your top six strengths played a role in your life successes?
- What effect do your top strengths have on others?
- How do your top strengths help you?
- Which aspects of your daily activities or job draw on your strengths?
- Which aspects squash them?
- How could you spend more of your time and energy doing what you do best?
- Are there any changes you can make to use your strengths each day?
- What do you do regularly that drains your energy? And how can you minimize that?
- What do you do regularly that energizes you? And how can you maximize that?

VIEW YOUR STRENGTHS FROM TOP TO BOTTOM

Take a look at the order of your strengths as produced by the VIA survey. Your middle strengths tend to be used in some situations (for example, at work but not at home), whereas your top strengths tend to be used in most situations. The last (approximately five) strengths are those that you may use in a few situations. They tend not to come as easily and naturally as the others, they take more effort and drain your energy, whereas the top strengths will energize you.

Strengths can be developed if you choose. If you feel there is a strength that is underused and is detrimental to yourself, or others, then you may choose to be mindful and learn to develop it within yourself until it comes naturally. For example, self-regulation is now one of my top strengths, but I had to choose to develop it and have refined it over the years. I began to learn it when I practised meditation as a child, but I honed the skill when I did a degree via The Open University.

I was living in the middle of the Welsh mountains (pre-internet days) with no radio or television signal (both of which I needed to study via The Open University). I was a single mother so I had to be very disciplined to make myself study every night once my son had gone to bed. I spent six years developing self-regulation by doing the degree on my own, apart from the one week each year when I went to the Summer School. It is a strength that I value because I know it has enabled me to achieve a lot of my goals.

Spotting Strengths

Being aware of and using your strengths will help increase your understanding and perception of yourself, which results in an improvement of your self-esteem and self-compassion. It helps clarify a sense of self and identity. The more you understand yourself, the more you are able to understand others. Being able to spot strengths within yourself gives you a greater ability to recognize strengths in those around you.

It is wonderful to develop your ability to spot other people's strengths. The more you recognize and appreciate other people's strengths, the more you see people in a positive light and the more gratitude you feel toward them for what they bring to different situations.

This increase in positivity and gratitude will also increase your happiness, as we have seen in the Positivity and Gratitude chapters. It will also improve your relationships with people, whether they are colleagues, friends, romantic partners or neighbours.

Understanding strengths can often provide a lens through which we see the world, as well as the way we understand people and situations. It affects what we believe is valuable and important, which affects our emotional response to things and shapes our behaviour. To sum it up, it is key to understanding ourselves as well as others, which in turn leads to greater life satisfaction and happiness.

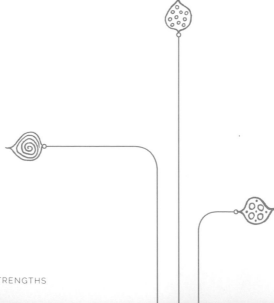

Try It Out:
See It in Others

Think of someone you admire – this may be a person you know, a famous person or a historical figure. Write down what it is about this person that you admire. What are the qualities within them that you are drawn to? Use the VIA Classification of Strengths to write down the strengths this person has.

• Do you share any of those strengths? If so, which ones?

The ones that you don't share – are these strengths you would like to develop within yourself or simply appreciate in others? Remember you can develop any strength you choose if you focus on it – this also refers back to having a growth mindset (see page 30).

Now try the following:

• Think of a loved one – family or partner – and write down their strengths.
• Think of someone you find difficult – it is best to use someone you know in real life – and write down their strengths.

Spotting strengths in people we don't know or find difficult may take more thought than for people we admire and love. But, the point is, everyone has character strengths – the skill is that you are able to see these qualities and appreciate them.

The more you do this, not only will your relationships improve, but you may find you become more discerning about who you ask for help, or do different things with. In other words, you may be more mindful of matching the strengths with the activity when it comes to others as well as yourself.

Case Study:
Dear Prudence

After attending one of my workshops, a woman sat with her son at home and they both did the VIA Character Strengths Survey together. She was amazed that his top strength was prudence (being careful about one's choices; not taking undue risks; not saying or doing things that might later be regretted).

She said that for the first time, she was able to appreciate this aspect of her son that she had always been quite frustrated by. She would get annoyed with him when he asked her what route she was taking for her daily hike (they lived in a remote area), and he'd always tell her to be careful and ask what time she expected to be back.

However, following the VIA survey, she heard his questions in a different light, and she automatically stopped being so irritated by them. Comprehending his top strength enabled her to have a different understanding and new appreciation of him. She particularly appreciated his strength of prudence when he asked if he could go on his first holiday with his mates abroad. She felt comfortable giving her approval for him to go and have a good time.

The Top Benefits of Awareness of Strengths

As you become more aware of your strengths, you will notice:

- Greater happiness
- Improved relationships
- Improved energy levels
- More smiling
- More laughing
- Increased life satisfaction
- More fulfilment
- Increased self-esteem
- Greater appreciation of self
- Greater appreciation of others
- Greater empowerment
- Decreased anger
- Decreased stress
- Decreased worry
- Less depression
- Less anxiety
- Greater motivation
- Greater meaning at work
- Greater engagement

CHAPTER 6

Hope

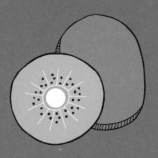

Shane Lopez is a scientist and world-leading hope researcher. He defines hope as the "belief that the future will be better than the present, along with the belief that you have the power to make it so."

Hope is often misunderstood. It is not unusual to think of it in terms of "I hope such and such happens", as though it's a pipedream or wishful thinking, but there is a significant difference between wishful thinking and hope.

Wishful thinking is passive. We "wish" something to happen but we don't necessarily do anything further than simply wishing for it. Hope, on the other hand, is *active*, so when we hope for something to happen, we work out the steps we need to take in order to make it happen.

Another difference between the two is the potential negative or positive reinforcement. In other words, if we *wish* for something and it doesn't happen when we believed it would, it can have the negative effect of undermining our confidence and our belief that things will get better or change. The more this happens, the more it reinforces a negative belief and erodes our confidence. This negative effect happens regardless of whether the person actually did anything to change their circumstance or make the wish happen.

Similarly, if it does happen that too can be disempowering if we think that it happened because of a *wish* rather than anything we did.

However, if you *hope* for something and it does happen, it has the positive effect of building your confidence in your ability to make things happen and have some control over your life. Therefore, hope is empowering which, in turn, will positively reinforce the idea that you do indeed have the power to make positive changes in your life. This will have a good effect on both you and those around you.

And if it doesn't happen, then that too can be beneficial as a learning opportunity, if you break down what happened to understand why and therefore what you can do differently next time.

For example, if you *wish* for more money yet nothing changes, it can reinforce feelings of powerlessness. However, if you *hope* for money you will work out steps to achieve your goal, such as training, writing a CV and searching for a new job.

Hope for the Future

Ask yourself: do you believe the future will be as good, or better, than the present? Do you believe you have some power/control over making your future better?

The key points here are the belief that the future will be better than the present – this is the first half of hope. If you don't believe the future can, or will, be better than the present then you are unlikely to strive for anything, hence the term "hopeless". Hopelessness is an awful state to be in and it is often correlated with depression.

The second half of hope is the belief that you have the power or control to enable a better future. If you feel powerless that you have no control, then lethargy and depression can set in. Hope is what helps us see the light at the end of the tunnel, even if it is a very long tunnel.

As discussed in the chapter on Positivity (see page 86), there are significant benefits when we shift our minds to a positive mindset and believe that the future will be better than the present – our minds will broaden and build. Our thoughts are also more creative when we have a positive mindset, and that includes being able to find solutions to even the most difficult problems or situations. It is those wonderfully positive hopeful thoughts that enable you to have the belief that you can make things happen.

A key difference between people with high hope and low hope is long- and short-term thinking. Low-hope people are more inclined to think in the short term. For example, they are more likely to make unhealthy choices, as they are thinking about short-term pleasure rather than long-term consequence. Whereas high-hope people think in the long term, and are more likely to make choices affected by long-term goals.

The Schools of Hope

I am a trustee for an amazing small charity called The Rahula Trust. The charity was started 20 years ago and is run by Buddhist monks and other volunteers. It sponsors children in poverty to help them stay in education, and all the money raised goes to the children.

In 2017, I joined Venerable Bandula, who runs the charity, on his annual trip to visit some of the children in Sri Lanka, who are supported by the Trust. I watched the youngsters as they came one by one to show Venerable Bandula their school reports, starting with the little ones who were around six years old and ending with two of the eldest. These two older students were actually no longer children – one was a 20-year-old man who had just finished a physics degree at university and the other an 18-year-old woman who was just about to go to university.

If there was any child there that day who arrived with low hope, they were filled with hope as they listened to the two older students tell their stories. All the children came from the same area and most had been sponsored by the Trust from the age of six. Here were two of them grown up, one about to start university and the other planning to go on to do a PhD. I could barely contain my emotion.

The point is, even in the most extreme situations, we can have or develop hope for our future. We can see that we have power and control, even if we tend to underestimate just how much we have.

Sometimes we subconsciously underestimate how much control we have, as it is seemingly easier if we feel we don't have to do anything about our situation. However, we can fall into the victim role. It can seem like a harder choice to take responsibility for our own future and acknowledge that we do have the power to change it. However, the moment you recognize that, you will feel empowered, hopeful and more positive.

Three Ways to Hope

The three factors that make up the second half of hope need to be considered – goals, pathways and agents of change. You need all three to make the things you are hoping for materialize. Let's break it down:

GOALS

This is where you want to get to, or what you want to achieve. Goals can be either short term or long term, and you can have relatively small, short-term goals and massively ambitious, long-term goals running concurrently in your mind.

Ideally, having goals is an enjoyable experience – we have fun and get excited imagining and talking about what our goals are, as well as what the journey is going to be like and how it will be when we get there. However, we need to be mindful to ensure our goals do not become pressures, which could be destructive.

Watch Out

Sometimes goals can become pressures when they are not really our goals, but are situations or outcomes we think we "should" adopt, or were put upon us. Watch out as we can internalize goals that other people impose on us. Classically, this can be a parent or caregiver, and it can be difficult to distinguish our own voices from theirs.

If you do feel overwhelmed by a goal, then ask yourself if it is really your goal and your hope for your future. If it isn't, then see it for what it is and begin to let it go. On the other hand, if it does feel like a good fit, then scale it down so it doesn't feel so overwhelming and too much. This leads us on to the next factor of pathways.

PATHWAYS

These are the various routes we can take to realize our goal, and are full of creative ideas for taking each step to where we want to be. A positive, hopeful mindset will enable us to be flexible in our thinking and to adapt and change along the way when it is necessary.

It's important to write and/or draw what the pathway is and what it consists of, including all the steps and signposts. The more creative you can be with this the better – this is explained further on page 153.

AGENTS OF CHANGE

The image that comes to mind when I think of this term is a special agent – strong, powerful and dynamic! We are our own agents of change and we need to take responsibility for our change and go forward with our inner strength, energy, determination and resilience (see the chapter on Resilience, page 102). Energy is the key factor here, as nothing will happen if we have a goal and know the pathway but don't have the energy to do it.

PUTTING THEM TOGETHER

We need the energy to make our goals and pathways happen. I might have the goal to climb Mount Everest, and I can work out the pathways to achieve it, but I need to want it enough to put in the required energy and time to achieve it.

All three factors need to be balanced and tended to in order to achieve the desired goals. Each interacts with the others – reinforcing, modifying or diminishing. You need to be mindful of them to ensure they are doing what you would like them to do.

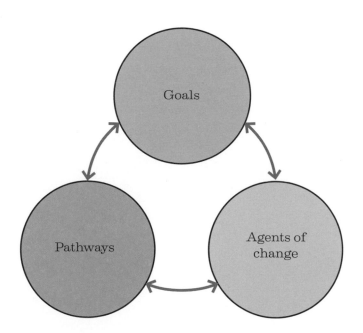

Meaning and Motivation

Meaning and motivation (M&M) are important for hope and give you the energy and drive needed for it. This will be discussed further in the Meaning and Motivation chapter (see page 162). M&Ms are likely to be different for each goal – you need to ask yourself and be clear about what your M&Ms are for each goal.

As you progress along the path to achieving the goal, your M&Ms may change and you'll need to be mindful of those shifts along the way. For example, a client wanted to lose weight for an upcoming wedding and her M&M was to look good on the day. However, as she progressed and began to lose weight, her confidence began to grow and her M&M changed into a deeper, more significant goal of wanting to look and feel good as a whole, way beyond the wedding. The initial M&M changed into her wanting to live a healthy, happy lifestyle where she became proud of taking care of her wellbeing.

Try It Out: Preparing for Hope

Write down the most significant thing you have achieved in the last year or so. In your mind, rewind to five years before this significant thing and write down detailed answers to the following five questions:

1. Five years ago, did you think you would have achieved this significant thing?

2. What did it take to achieve it in terms of energy, determination and resilience?

3. What were the pathways?

4. What obstacles did you encounter and overcome?

5. What were your meanings and motivations?

Read the following notes on each of the above questions *after* you have done the exercise:

1. The purpose of this question becomes clear when you are preparing to set another new goal, particularly a big goal. It is helpful to remember, acknowledge and recognize how likely success seemed five years prior to your recent achievement – more often than not clients tell me five years ago they never would have believed it if someone said it would happen. This realization helps build confidence (no matter how unlikely it might seem at the present) that you can achieve the new goal too.

2. Once people achieve a goal, they often forget just how much time, effort, tenacity and resilience it took to achieve it. It's only when we reflect, that we remember. This helps prepare us for the next goal.

3. It's helpful to recall what the pathways were to remind yourself of how you achieved the goal. This is empowering as you recall how you did it, even if your new goal is very different.

4. Recalling the dead ends and difficulties that you encountered and how you overcame them helps you recognize that you have tackled many obstacles before and you are able to create alternative routes to get to a destination. This builds your resilience and stops you being derailed by obstacles. People with high hope are more liable to think of obstacles as challenges that they enjoy working out.

5. Meaning and motivation are what give you energy and drive to keep you moving forward (discussed in more detail on the following pages and in the Meaning and Motivation chapter).

You Can See Your Goals

Our brains are amazing things. The hippocampus and the prefrontal cortex are two parts of the brain that are essential for hope (both will benefit when you practise meditation). They are our experience simulators which enable us to visualize and plan our future.

In fact, visualization is crucial here because, as discussed in the first chapter (see page 38), the brain can't distinguish between real and imagined events. The hippocampus and prefrontal cortex access our memories, experiences and knowledge, all of which are essential for setting goals, creating pathways and building agency. Naturally, it is our past experience and knowledge that help inform our decision-making and goal-setting.

Imagine completing your goal. Where are you? Is there anyone with you or are you alone? How do you feel? How do you look? How are you dressed? What are you doing?

Enjoy getting a clear picture in your mind – the clearer the images, the more power they will have to affect your choices. That can be experienced in many different ways – for example, if you visualize being in your dream job then you are more likely to choose to do the work needed to get yourself there.

With a clear picture of your goal in mind, it's time to get focused about how you are going to achieve it. That is, you need to think about your pathways.

You can write down, mind-map, draw or collect pictures of what those pathways might look like. Cut out images from magazines or brochures, or download pictures from the internet (Pinterest is helpful for this). Choose whatever way is right for you, and always try to have fun as you work out the best route. Make note of the signposts you may see along your journey. Signposts are helpful marker points that let you know where you are along the path, much like the marker points along a marathon route that tell the runners how far they've run to help keep them going.

When thinking about pathways, it also helps to break down the big goals into a series of small goals (these then become your signposts). This will give you an ongoing sense of achievement as you meet each step along the way to the end goal.

However, it's important to allow yourself to modify your goals when necessary – beware of being too rigid. I always turn to nature for guidance – if you look at a river you will see it is formed through consistent effort and ends up bending and curving round obstacles – you will never see a river that is perfectly straight. Those curves are part of what makes a river beautiful.

Try to sense when to bend around an obstacle rather than keep banging against it in the hope it will give way. Let go of the expectation that the journey will be a straight line – there may be patches of straight and then you'll gracefully curve round a challenge. Similarly, there are times when bending round takes us in a different direction altogether – it's all about being mentally flexible and open to those possibilities.

It's also good to know there will be times when a block will actually lead to a wonderful opportunity, which we may never have encountered otherwise. Life is full of unexpected opportunities but we have to be open to recognizing them and seizing them.

For example, I had an Italian client who had come to Bath to study architecture. She got a good job in an architectural practice and fell in love with a guy from Bath. They ended up living together and for about five years life was great. However, her life came crashing down when he ended the relationship and soon after she was made redundant. She was at a total loss and came to see me for help.

There was no work in Italy at that time so going back wasn't really an option. After a few months of therapy, her confidence and hope were restored and she decided to have the gap year she'd never had. She went off to Africa full of excitement and open to what opportunities might come. That was about ten years ago – she is now living in New Zealand, she has her own architectural practice, is happily married and has two beautiful children.

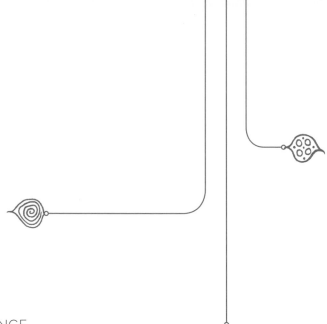

SEE THE CHALLENGE

Some obstacles or challenges are more predictable than others. It can be helpful to visualize how you would overcome and resolve challenges that you think may arise. For example, if your goal is to stop drinking alcohol then it would be helpful to visualize being in a social situation where everyone else is drinking.

This gives you the opportunity to pre-empt the situation and create solutions to help you overcome the challenge, if and when it does arise. With your experience simulator (your amazing brain) you can visualize the various scenarios where you are confronted with difficulties and then see yourself dealing with them in a skilful way, rather than acting in a way you may regret, because you didn't have the time to prepare for it mentally. It will also reduce any fear you may have of being confronted by certain situations.

Once you've created a picture of your goals, pathways and signposts then the last thing to clarify is your agency.

BE AN AGENT OF CHANGE

What image comes to mind when you see yourself as your own agent of change? The Pink Panther, Superwoman, James Bond? Have fun seeing yourself as a special agent of change.

What empowers you? What gives you the energy to embark on this journey? Is this the right time? In other words, have you got the time and energy to do it at this point in your life?

This is where meaning and motivation come in again – you need to be aware of what they are as that is what gives you energy and drive, particularly when you are having a bad day. It's what keeps you going when you feel like giving up.

Try It Out: Goal Scoring

Write down why one of your goals is important to you.

• What would it mean to achieve it?

• How does it fit in with your values, passions and identity?

The clearer you are about these things, the more energized you will be. See the Meaning and Motivation chapter (page 162) to explore this further.

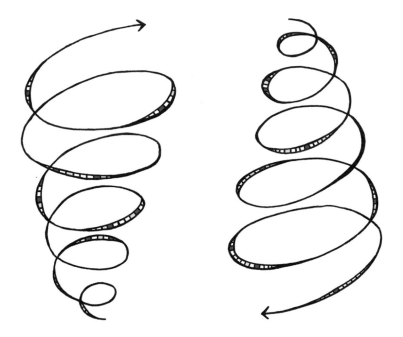

Watch Out

A potential pitfall for people with low hope is overestimating what they can achieve and so, inevitably, setting themselves up for failure. This is a form of self-sabotage in the sense that if they don't succeed then it reinforces the idea that they are not good enough. Common phrases can be: "I always fail", "I never succeed", "I can't ever do anything" and "I'll always be a failure". The way to counteract this is by making sure the goal, pathways and agency are realistic.

It's best to set small goals, even if you think they are too small. That way each goal you achieve will build your confidence and set things going upward in a positive spiral with positive reinforcement, as opposed to the negative spiral with negative reinforcement, which undermines confidence and hope.

Go with the Flow

You don't *always* need to have a goal in mind to be hopeful. There are times in life when it's appropriate to let go and see where life takes you – again it's all about balance.

If you've always had a goal and been very driven by goals, then it's good to take the pressure off and have time without them. Just let go and let life be. However, if you're not prone to setting goals for yourself and you drift along seeing whether things happen (or not) without you directing it, then setting some goals would be a good thing.

The key is not to swing to either extreme, but to find a balance where some things in your life are goal driven, while others are not.

Reinhold Niebuhr's serenity prayer says it perfectly:

> *"Grant me the serenity to accept the things I cannot change, the courage to change the things I can, and the wisdom to know the difference."*

Although it might seem like a cliché to say "enjoy the journey", it is really important that you do enjoy the journey. When you think about how much time a journey might take, and the fact that we are on one journey or another for most of our lives, it is vital that we enjoy it.

When people reflect back on their journey, they often say "Getting there ended up being the fun bit", and they regret not realizing that at the time. However, if you are mindful, and in the moment, then you will enjoy every step of the way anyway.

Hope You Feel Better Soon

One study, conducted in 2007, examined how hope affected children when it came to taking asthma medication. They measured the children's hope levels at the beginning of the study and then measured their compliance in taking their medication.

The study showed that each child's level of hope predicted whether they took the medication or not. Hope affects many choices we make in the present and determines how we take care of ourselves on every level – our physical wellbeing, psychological wellbeing and future lifestyle wellbeing.

The Top Benefits of Hope

More hope in your life:
- Leads to greater success in a variety of spheres
- Improves academic performance
- Predicts grades, performance and absenteeism
- Predicts ongoing enrolment and graduation better than normal entrance examinations
- Increases workplace productivity
- Reduces workplace absenteeism
- Predicts athletic outcomes better than other variables including athletic ability
- Increases happiness
- Increases tolerance to pain
- Reduces depression and anxiety

CHAPTER 7

Meaning and Motivation

Meaning and motivation (M&M) are the driving forces behind what we do. They give us the energy and drive to fulfil our goals, whatever they may be. Meaning and motivation push us forward, giving us the oomph, the vitality and the tenacity to keep going, even on the difficult days. They give our life greater purpose, which is another key factor for life satisfaction.

Meaning, in this context, is related to life purpose and what underlies our actions, usually referring to a purpose or passion greater than ourselves. The dictionary definition of motivation is "a reason, or reasons, for acting or behaving in a particular way. Willingness to do something, or something that causes such willingness."

The way I see it, knowing the meaning behind what we do gives us the motivation to do it. This is why I see them as inextricably linked.

Meaning → motivation → momentum

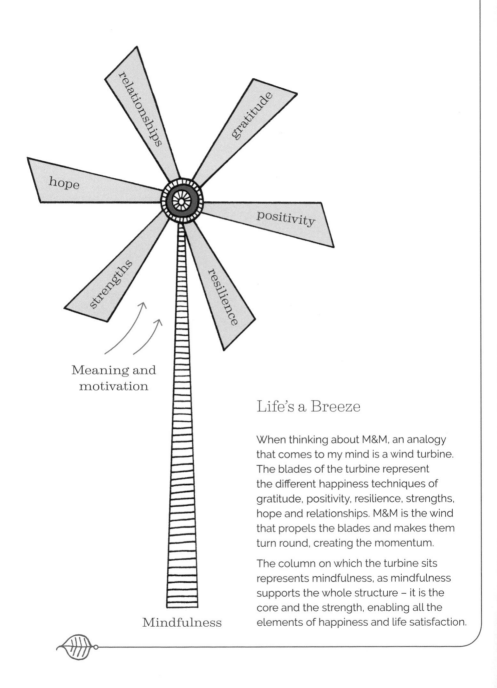

relationships

gratitude

hope

positivity

strengths

resilience

Meaning and
motivation

Mindfulness

Life's a Breeze

When thinking about M&M, an analogy
that comes to my mind is a wind turbine.
The blades of the turbine represent
the different happiness techniques of
gratitude, positivity, resilience, strengths,
hope and relationships. M&M is the wind
that propels the blades and makes them
turn round, creating the momentum.

The column on which the turbine sits
represents mindfulness, as mindfulness
supports the whole structure – it is the
core and the strength, enabling all the
elements of happiness and life satisfaction.

Know Your M&Ms

It's important to be aware of what the M&Ms are in the different aspects of your life. They could be the same across all aspects, but for most of us they change according to context, such as professional or personal. We may have one overarching M&M and then different ones for each separate goal within that.

For example, the overarching meaning for your work might be to protect the environment. However, within your work there could be different aspects which lead to that goal, either directly or indirectly. It is therefore important to understand the meaning behind each of those aspects.

Another example could be that a student's meaning may be their passion for animal welfare, and that is what gives them the motivation to do a degree in veterinary medicine. Each assignment has the same overarching M&M, but to get through the long and difficult degree, they have to be clear about their goal for each individual assignment, as well as the overarching M&M.

Remember, there is no right or wrong. It's all about understanding what drives you and what is important to you in the different areas of your life.

Try It Out:
What Drives You?

Think of one area of your life – this could be work, family, romantic partner, friends, spiritual life, hobbies, voluntary work or exercise. Now write down the answers to the following questions:

• Why is it important to you?

• What is the M&M behind what you do? And why is it important to you?

• Is that M&M a significant enough driving force on bad days? If not, then you need to find one that is (see page 175).

WHAT MAKES THE WORLD GO ROUND?

There are endless examples of M&M. Here are just a few:

• Gender equality, feminism, the "Me Too" Movement

• Racial equality, civil rights, ending discrimination

• Environment, climate change, recycling, plastic pollution

• Religion, spirituality, philosophy

• Family, loved ones, friends

Don't worry if you don't know what your M&Ms are at the moment – hopefully by the end of this chapter you will have a clearer idea. Some people know from an early age what their M&Ms are, but for most people they emerge as they progress through life. They usually change as we mature and develop different interests and passions. What motivates us at the age of ten is unlikely to be the same as what motivates us at 30, and so on. Also M&Ms change as our life circumstances change – the most obvious example of this is becoming a parent.

The philosopher Nietzsche said:

> *"A man who has a why to live for can bear with almost any how."*

One of the most powerful examples of knowing your M&Ms comes from the psychiatrist Victor Frankl, a Holocaust survivor. I highly recommend his book *Man's Search For Meaning* in which he discusses his experiences in the camps and his theory that people's desire for meaning was more directly related to their survival than anything else. The meaning and motivations that Frankl used to help him survive were the thought of his wife (he didn't know whether she was alive or not), the goal of writing his book and lecturing about the psychology of being in a concentration camp. Sadly, Frankl was to learn his wife had not survived, but after the war he did manage to write, lecture and develop his theory.

QUESTION THE "WHY"

Whatever you currently do or have as a goal to do, try to be clear about what your meaning and motivation is. Ask yourself:

• Why are you doing it?

• Why is it important to you?

• What does it mean to you (or what will it mean to you)?

• Are you passionate about it? If so, what is it about it that makes you passionate?

• How does it make you feel?

• How does it fit into the bigger picture in terms of your life's purpose?

The life of the activist Malala offers a great example of resilience and tenacity driven by meaning and motivation. She was brought up in Pakistan by a father who wanted her to have the same opportunities as a boy. However, when she was ten, the Taliban took control of the Swat Valley (where she lived) and a year later they banned girls from attending school. At this point Malala felt compelled to speak out about what was happening, and the meaning and motivation that would drive her life was formed.

She began writing a blog for the BBC, talking about education for girls and what life was like under the Taliban. She also went on to make a documentary for *The New York Times* and a few years later won Pakistan's National Youth Peace Prize. Around this time the Taliban had been forced out of the Swat Valley and girls, including Malala, were able to go back to school. However, because she had spoken out against the Taliban they targeted her, boarded her school bus and shot her in the head, neck and shoulder. She was only 15 years old.

Fortunately she survived. A few months after being shot, she was brought to the UK for treatment. Since her recovery she has continued to dedicate her life to raising awareness of the importance of girls' education, to give all girls access to education and equality around the world. She went on to set up the Malala Fund, publish a book, win the Nobel Peace Prize at the age of 17 (the youngest person ever to receive the prize) and has spoken to some of the most influential people in the world to achieve her goals.

On her 16th birthday she gave a speech to the United Nations in which she said, "They thought that the bullets would silence us, but they failed. And out of that silence came thousands of voices. The terrorists thought they would change my aims and stop my ambitions. But nothing changed in my life except this: weakness, fear and hopelessness died. Strength, power and courage were born."

The lives of Victor Frankl and Malala demonstrate two amazing (and extreme) examples of M&M, but M&M can be found in everything we do. I love the parable of the three bricklayers. When a man asked them one by one what they were doing, the first bricklayer said he was laying bricks; the second one said he was building a wall; and the third one said he was building a cathedral. The first one had a job, the second a career and the third had M&M. You can imagine who was the most likely to possess satisfaction in his job and his life as a whole – the key is the meaning you give to what you do, not the job title or anything else.

Being clear about your M&Ms gives you the resilience to keep going, and research shows that it increases life satisfaction throughout your years. So maybe you need to make some changes, perhaps to your job or career. Sometimes, however, the change that is needed is *how* you work. How would you do your job differently, in order to make it more meaningful to you? I would even suggest you mention your ideas to your boss – the business case for allowing you to make this change is that it will make you happier, more engaged and passionate about your job. This is called "job crafting" and is often done in large companies such as Google.

How to Find Your M&Ms #1: Get Inspired

A simple starting point for discovering your M&Ms is to explore what you are interested in, what makes you feel passionate, fired up, angry, upset, energized – in other words, what you care about. Read articles and books on different subjects, listen to TED Talks, watch documentaries and films and notice what you want to know more about. Start to form a picture of what your subjects are, finding the initial spark of interest and nurturing it.

You can then connect these to your strengths and values (look back at your signature strengths discussed on page 132). Ideally you want to do things that are in harmony with your authentic self, your values and strengths and to lead a life that reflects who you are. Think about what values you want to live your life by and why these values are important to you. For example, if compassion is important, every compassionate act you do can bring meaning, no matter how small. Life is made up of small actions.

How to Find Your M&Ms #2: Write from Within

Take a piece of paper and write at the top: **"Meaning and motivation for my…"**

Now fill in the rest. You may want to explore the M&Ms for your whole life or just a particular area of your life. Write whatever comes to mind, and try not to think too hard about it. Ideally you want it come from a deeper place within you, beyond your conscious, intellectual self.

M&Ms come from our emotional self. There are times when our intellectual self can get in the way and block us, putting in obstacles which might come from our insecurities or internalized voices of unhelpful people in our past or present life – for example, when a parent told us as a child that we were not good at a certain thing or minimized our dreams by telling us to "be realistic".

Free yourself by allowing yourself to write whatever ideas come to mind, whether the conscious mind tells you they are unrealistic, seemingly crazy or otherwise. Just write and see what comes up when you tap into your heart and give it a voice.

Notice if anything triggers an emotional reaction. If you wish, afterwards you can think about why that emotion was triggered (this will also offer greater insight into aspects of yourself). But, for now, let yourself write for long enough that you tap into that deeper part of yourself and unlock your true M&Ms (and not the ones that society, culture or family might have imposed upon you).

It is wonderful what amazing M&Ms arise when we give ourselves permission to unshackle ourselves.

How to Find Your M&Ms #3: Write Your Eulogy

Another great way to find more clarity with your M&Ms is to write your eulogy. Contemplate what is important to you.

• How do you want people to remember you when you are gone?

• What would you love people to say about you?

• How do you want to impact your loved ones, family, friends and any other people in your life?

• What would you love to accomplish in your lifetime?

• What legacy will you leave?

• If you reflect back on your life what would you look at with pride?

This is a really helpful exercise, because as well as helping us think about what our M&Ms are, it helps us put things into perspective as we think about our own impermanence. In this way we can contemplate what is important and what is not. We often get caught up in the small stuff in life and thinking about death is a great way to remind us what is actually important and what isn't worth worrying about.

Is there anything you think you would wish you had spent more time doing? Also thinking about how much time we still have to complete our hopes and dreams can nudge or jolt us into action. Drawing a life timeline – birth to death – and marking where you think you are now can be a real wake-up call.

How to Find Your M&Ms #4: Inspiration from Others

Think of someone who inspires you and write down what it is you are drawn to. Role models can help inspire us and develop those same qualities within ourselves. Try connecting with others who have the same interests and passions. Find ways to volunteer and get involved so you can find out if this is an M&M for you (see page 218 for a list of suggested voluntary organizations).

True Grit

The psychologist Angela Duckworth carried out research on high achievers to uncover what enabled their success. She concluded it was not high IQ, high exam grades or top university degrees, but that "it was this combination of passion and perseverance that made high achievers special." She labelled this as "grit". She has done a fantastic TED Talk and book, both of which I recommend.

The terminology might be different, but passion and perseverance are basically the same as meaning and motivation. Duckworth explains that what we accomplish depends more on our passion and perseverance than our innate talent. People have a subconscious bias toward innate talent, choosing people who are "naturals" over people who have striven for their success, even though, on a conscious level, they may say they value hard work over natural talent.

Duckworth said that without effort, talent is nothing more than unmet potential. Effort is doubly important.

Talent × effort = skill

Skill × effort = achievement

When you are passionate about your subject, you put in the effort required to achieve your goal. You want to learn, develop, improve and stretch yourself. You also find it is energizing and you are more liable to get into "flow" (another interesting subject to read about when you have time).

People who are clear about their M&Ms often say they would continue working in their field even if they won the lottery. It is not simply talent or intelligence that determines success, it is M&M, passion, perseverance – in Duckworth's words, it is grit.

I'd like to end this section with one final comment about the way motivation changes. As people pursue goals, such as losing weight, getting fit, eating healthy food and saving money, this is known as "promotion motivation". With promotion motivation, reaching a desired positive outcome drives us. However, when people are close to their goal this can change to "prevention motivation". This is when we are driven by the desire to avoid a negative outcome – for example, putting weight back on or losing the fitness we've built up.

It is good to be aware of how far along you are with your goals, but also be aware of whether you are in promotion or prevention mode. Are you at a point where it would be helpful to consciously shift from one to the other? Being conscious of that switch will help you maintain motivation and achieve your goals.

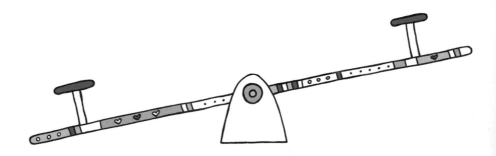

The Top Benefits of Meaning & Motivation

Improving your meaning and motivation will lead to:

- Increased life satisfaction
- Increased positive emotions
- Increased optimism
- Increased self-esteem
- Increased health
- Increased longevity
- Increased tenacity
- Increased energy

CHAPTER **8**

Relationships

Relationships are crucial to our happiness and wellbeing. Human beings are social creatures who need connections and thrive from them. Our evolution and survival have relied upon living in groups, so it is hard-wired within us.

Lasting over 75 years, one of the longest studies of adult life ever conducted was Harvard's Grant and Glueck study. Running from 1938 to 2014, the study looked at the physical and mental health of 456 people from the underprivileged part of Boston (the study started during the Great Depression) and 268 Harvard students. Over time, the study expanded to include the wives and children of the participants.

Robert Waldinger, the director of the study, discovered that our level of happiness within our relationships has a powerful influence on our health. The research revealed that close, happy relationships are better predictors of a long and happy life than social class, money, fame, IQ and genes. Waldinger said: "When we gathered together everything we knew about [the participants] at age 50, it wasn't their middle-age cholesterol levels that predicted how they were going to grow old. It was how satisfied they were in their relationships. The people who were the most satisfied in their relationships at age 50 were the healthiest at age 80."

He asserted that, "Loneliness kills. It's as powerful as smoking and alcoholism." Participants with good relationships and social support had less mental deterioration, less depression and better memory function. The previous director of the study, George Vaillant, commented, "When the study began, nobody cared about empathy or attachment. But the key to healthy ageing is relationships." Naturally, however, this doesn't mean that a good relationship can override an unhealthy life.

Vaillant listed six factors that can predict healthy ageing:

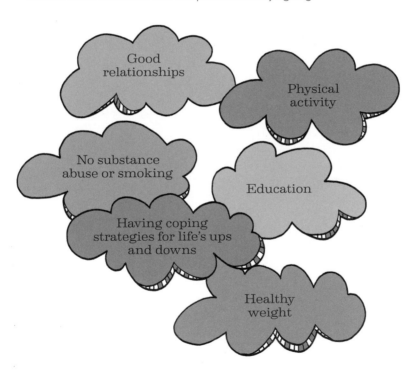

It's important to note that good and happy relationships involve feeling connected to family, friends, neighbours and work colleagues who you can trust and will be there for you when you need them. It's not the quantity that counts, but it's the quality of the relationships that makes the difference.

It Starts with You

Before you focus on your relationships with other people, you need to focus on your relationship with yourself. This is the first and most crucial relationship. Ideally, you want to like – and even love – yourself. When we start to generate self-compassion within ourselves, compassion naturally radiates out toward everyone else we have a relationship with. When we focus on filling our inner core with self-compassion, eventually it will begin to overflow and that overflow is what goes out to others – you will soon give happily and with an open heart.

However, when we give to others but not to ourselves we can feel resentful and have conditions, attachments and expectations around our giving, all of which can result in upset and negative feelings. Compassion Meditation (see page 69) is a wonderful way to develop self-compassion. Research shows that practising mindfulness also increases self-compassion.

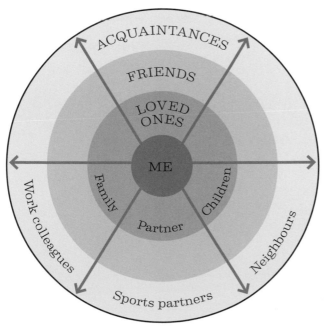

WHAT IS SELF-COMPASSION?

Self-compassion is the ability to have compassion toward ourselves whatever the situation. While this might sound obvious (and, even possibly, easy), as discussed elsewhere in the book, our inner dialogue can often be harsh. More often than not, we are much harder with ourselves than we would be to a friend or even a stranger. Self-compassion enables us to respond to ourselves in the way we would to a best friend – in a loving, caring, considerate, supportive, reassuring, helpful, encouraging way, as opposed to a response that is intolerant, impatient, judgemental, accusatory and unkind.

Two common misperceptions of inner dialogue are that being harsh is the best way to motivate ourselves, also that we are being selfish if we develop self-compassion. However, the science tells us that neither of these is the case. Self-criticism and feeling inadequate are entwined with depression and anxiety – people who are more self-compassionate are less anxious and less depressed. Self-compassion is recognized as being a protective factor for anxiety and depression. Needless to say, depression and anxiety are not states associated with motivation and selflessness.

Research shows that people who practise self-compassion have fewer negative emotions, such as fear, irritability, hostility and distress. Self-compassion also helps lessen the cycle of negative rumination and is associated with happiness, optimism, positive effect and conscientiousness.

Kristin Neff, the leading self-compassion researcher, defined the following three components of self-compassion:

• Self-kindness vs self-judgement

• Common humanity vs isolation

• Mindfulness vs over-identification

Self-kindness vs Self-judgement

This is the difference between how we would talk to a friend compared to the self-critical, judgemental inner voice that we might apply to ourselves. This can happen so automatically that we can often be unaware of it, therefore the more we practise mindfulness, the more we will become aware of our inner voice, and mindfully make the shift to self-kindness.

Common Humanity vs Isolation

Common humanity is about the shared human experience – the fact that we all struggle, we all fail, we all make mistakes and life doesn't always go smoothly. However, when these things happen, it is common to feel we are the only ones in this situation, or ask "Why is this happening to me?" We feel as if we are the only one who failed, who messed up, who didn't succeed, and therefore we feel isolated. But, when we stop to think about it, we know everyone has these moments. The compassionate response is to recognize and acknowledge that what we are going through is part of the shared human experience. We can then have a gentle, kind and comforting reaction toward ourselves.

Mindfulness vs Over-Identification

Mindfulness allows us to observe our feelings and thoughts without judgement and to fully acknowledge them, as opposed to denying or suppressing them. (See the Mindful Observer's Perspective on page 119.) Sometimes, just acknowledging what you are feeling and thinking lessens the intensity of the thoughts and feelings. It also helps you to respond appropriately – next time, perhaps ask yourself, "What is the kindest thing I can do for myself right now?"

Over-identification is when we become consumed by thoughts, like the forest-fire analogy on page 120. Feelings and thoughts will pass by like the weather – we can stand back and observe or we can go into it. On a beautiful sunny day (positive emotions), we will naturally want to go out and absorb the warmth of the sun. But when there is a massive thunderstorm (negative emotions), it is wiser to stay inside and watch it pass.

The more you practise mindfulness, the more you will recognize that nothing is permanent, everything is subject to change – just like the weather. This helps us not to over-identify with negative emotions, but stand back and let them pass like a storm.

Try It Out:
Feel Your Way

Here is a self-compassion exercise to try now and to practise whenever you feel stressed, anxious or that things are not going to plan. At the end of the questions you will find what each of the steps relates to in terms of your levels of mindfulness, common humanity and self-compassion/self-kindness.

1. Think of something that is causing you stress, anxiety, worry or any other negative emotion.

2. Take note of how it makes you feel.

3. Where do you feel the distress in your body?

4. Say to yourself, "This is difficult/stressful [or whatever word is appropriate for you]".

5. Follow this by saying, "Difficulties are part of life, I'm not alone, this is a shared human experience [or whatever similar words work for you]".

6. Close your eyes and put your hands over the centre of your chest or anywhere else that is comforting (such as the belly).

7. Allow yourself to feel soothed.

8. Think about what you would say to a friend who was in the same situation as you.

9. Find those supportive, compassionate, kind words.

10. Finally ask yourself, "What do I need right now?"

11. Write down your answers to the various questions.

12. Take time to acknowledge and respond appropriately to the answers.

- Steps 2, 3 and 4 relate to mindfulness (noticing how you feel, where you feel it in the body and fully acknowledging it).
- Step 5 relates to common humanity.
- Steps 6 to 11 relate to self-compassion and self-kindness.

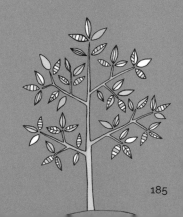

Kristin Neff's Self-compassion Scale

Take this test to get an understanding of your current levels of self-compassion.

Below are some statements about self-compassion. Please read each statement carefully before answering. Note down how you typically act toward yourself in difficult times, using the following scale:

Almost never   Neutral   Almost always

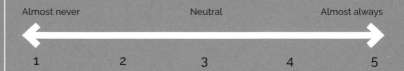

1   2   3   4   5

1. When I fail at something important to me, I become consumed by feelings of inadequacy.

2. I try to be understanding and patient toward those aspects of my personality I don't like.

3. When something painful happens, I try to take a balanced view of the situation.

4. When I'm feeling down, I tend to feel like most other people are probably happier than I am.

5. I try to see my failings as part of the human condition.

6. When I'm going through a very hard time, I give myself the caring and tenderness I need.

7. When something upsets me, I try to keep my emotions in balance.

8. When I fail at something that's important to me, I tend to feel alone in my failure.

9. When I'm feeling down, I tend to obsess and fixate on everything that's wrong.

10. When I feel inadequate in some way, I try to remind myself that feelings of inadequacy are shared by most people.

11. I'm disapproving and judgemental about my own flaws and inadequacies.

12. I'm intolerant and impatient toward those aspects of my personality I don't like.

- Add together the scores for statements 2, 3, 5, 6, 7 and 10.
- Reverse the scores for statements 1, 4, 8, 9, 11 and 12. (A score of 5 reverses to 1, 4 reverses to 2, 3 remains unchanged, 2 reverses to 4, 1 reverses to 5). Now add them together.
- Add together the two totals to get your overall score.

Interpreting Your Score on the Self-compassion Scale

Between 12 and 24
Low

You have a low self-compassion score, which indicates that you judge yourself harshly. You might find you get consumed by negative emotions and feel isolated in your experiences. This is a difficult place to be within oneself. Work on finding the words you would say to your best friend and apply them to yourself. Practise the Compassion Meditation (see page 69) to help you be kinder toward yourself.

Between 25 and 36
Average

You have an average self-compassion score, which indicates that you don't always judge yourself harshly, which is good. Try practising the Compassion Meditation (see page 69) and the previous self-compassion exercise (see page 185) to help you shift toward a more positive attitude to yourself. Redo the test after six months of practising to see if your score has improved.

Between 37 and 48
Good

You have a good self-compassion score, which indicates you are pretty good at being compassionate toward yourself. You might find it interesting to see your individual scores in each aspect to understand where you are doing really well and what might need a little attention to shift you into the amazing zone (see page 190). You are doing really well so keep being kind to yourself.

Between 49 and 60
Amazing

You have an amazing score. You are aware of the power of self-compassion and you practise it, which is fantastic. Keep doing what you are doing for yourself. Now would be a great time to start sending compassion out to others.

When you do the Compassion Meditation (see page 69) you can enjoy directing all that wonderful compassion to other people. Start by saying the phrases to yourself, then direct them to others. Just change the start of the phrases to suit the relevant person:

May [person you are sending it to] be happy

May [person you are sending it to] be healthy

May [person you are sending it to] have inner confidence

May [person you are sending it to] recognize and appreciate who he/she is

May [person you are sending it to] be peaceful

May [person you are sending it to] be joyful

Start by sending it to your loved ones, such as your family, children, parents or partners. Then send it to your friends, colleagues, neighbours and finally to people you find challenging. The last category can be difficult, but it is a wonderful way to positively change how you feel about someone, even the difficult people in your life.

INDIVIDUAL ASPECTS

If you want to get an indication of each aspect of the test, then total the score for each of the categories below (you do not need to reverse the scores for this part, just keep the original scores):

Self-kindness – statements 2 and 6

Common humanity – statements 5 and 10

Mindfulness – statements 3 and 7

Self-judgement – statements 11 and 12

Isolation – statements 4 and 8

Over-identification – statements 1 and 9

Ideally, you will have a high score (the top score for each category is 12) for self-kindness, common humanity and mindfulness, and a low score (the lowest score for each category is 2) for self-judgement, isolation and over-identification.

The Good in You

Self-criticism asks "Am I good enough?" while self-compassion asks "What's good for me?"

Self-compassion taps into our inner desire to be healthy and happy, valuing ourselves and making choices that lead to our wellbeing in the long term as well as the short term. There should be a balance between the two. If, for example, the most self-compassionate thing in the short term would be to stop working and relax, you need to consider whether you would put yourself under more pressure later by not getting the work done, affecting your wellbeing in the long term. Find the middle path, perhaps by having a relaxing break and then getting back to the work you need to do.

Research shows that self-esteem and self-compassion predict happiness, optimism and positivity. However, self-compassion predicts more stable feelings of self-worth than self-esteem. This difference could be due to self-esteem being more dependent on outcomes. Self-esteem can go up and down, depending on whether we feel things have gone well or not, but this is where self-compassion comes into its own. As discussed, a self-compassionate response when things do not work out is to comfort and help ourselves as we would a friend. This response is what enables people who practise self-compassion to have a different, and more positive, relationship with failure.

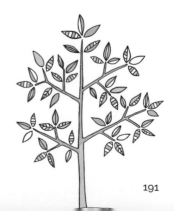

It is common for people to be averse to the feelings they have experienced with failure, particularly if they felt low self-esteem, low self-worth, shame, embarrassment, perhaps berating themselves for failing. These are such unpleasant feelings, that it is not surprising that people have a fear of failure, and get stuck in the perfectionism trap, shying away from situations that might result in any form of failure and the potential of feeling all those awful associated feelings. However, all that does is subconsciously reinforce the idea that they aren't good enough and that they shouldn't push themselves. Therefore, it becomes a self-fulfilling prophecy, as they don't find out whether they would succeed or not.

The more you practise self-compassion and let go of contingent self-esteem, the more you will encourage yourself to take a chance… and surprise yourself by discovering you can do it. By pushing yourself beyond your comfort zone, you will stretch yourself and grow. But if you stick within your comfort zone, then it will eventually become uncomfortable, as it constricts your growth more and more over time.

Self-compassion results in us becoming less afraid of failure. We will be more willing to accept it because we won't identify with it in the same way – we may say to ourselves, "Just because this failed doesn't mean I am a failure". I like the acronym FAIL: First Attempt In Learning, or Forever Acquiring Important Lessons.

Interestingly, the research also shows that those who practised self-compassion were not as affected by social comparison either – this is important in our current age of social media.

Building Bridges

As I've already discussed, each chapter in this book builds on the last – they are all interconnected. The reason relationships is the last chapter is because if you practise and develop all the other happiness skills then the relationships in every sphere of your life will improve.

The science shows that when each of the happiness skills is integrated into your life, it will have positive impact on your relationships. Here are just a few benefits:

- Gratitude results in focusing on what's good in a relationship.
- Gratitude increases reciprocity, which strengthens relationships with others.
- Mindfulness enables you to be mindful of yourself and others.
- Mindfulness enables self-compassion and compassion for others.
- Positivity keeps you away from the "Four Horsemen of the Apocalypse" (see page 196).
- Positivity fills your relationship "current account" as well as your relationship "savings account" (see page 198).
- Resilience helps you work through the tough times.
- Awareness of your strengths increases relationship satisfaction.
- Hope helps you enter into and stay in relationships.
- Hope gives you the joy and fun of shared goals.
- Meaning and motivation draw you, and bond you, to like-minded people.

Try It Out:
Five Ways To Strengthen Your Relationships

1. Write a gratitude letter to your partner (see page 56).

2. Say thank you in three ways (see page 53).

3. RAC – *Recognize*, *acknowledge* and *commend* each other's strengths. Ask your partner to complete the VIA Character Strengths test (see page 124), and discuss the results for both of you. Do you both agree with the top ten strengths? If not, discuss what you would change. Having learned each other's strengths, be mindful of spotting each other's strengths in action – openly recognize, acknowledge and commend each other's strengths. Be mindful of the different ways this exercise improves your relationship.

4. Enjoy creating shared goals. This can be great fun and bring hope and positivity into a relationship. Shared goals can be many things, such as choosing a holiday destination, an activity you both want to do, learning a new skill together, health goals, changing where you live, spiritual goals – the list is endless. Take time to create and plan a variety of big and smaller shared goals. When you carry out the goals you will also be creating lovely memories together, too. However, again, it's important to remember balance – while it's good to have shared goals, make sure you also have goals that are just for yourself.

5. Discuss and explore your M&Ms (see page 165). This exercise can deepen your relationship as you discuss what is meaningful and important to you. For example, what your belief systems are, your spiritual or religious beliefs and your political views. Take time to discuss your shared values. Needless to say balance is important here too – while it's not important that your partner and friends share all of your beliefs, there must be mutual respect of each other's values.

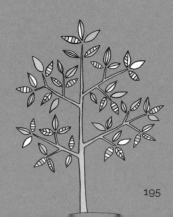

Make or Break

The "Four Horsemen of the Apocalypse" is what one of the world's leading relationship researchers, John Gottman, calls behaviours that have the potential to destroy a relationship. When he observes a couple and he sees the "Four Horsemen", he can predict the success or failure of a relationship with 82 per cent accuracy, and if he also sees a failure of repair attempts, this figure rises to 90 per cent. (Repair attempts are what Gottman calls the different ways people seek to remedy or de-escalate a difficult or conflict situation). The important point here is whether the other person responds positively to the attempt or not. Although Gottman's research focuses on what makes romantic relationships work (or break down), I believe his observations apply to most types of relationship. Throughout this chapter, when I use the term relationship I am also including those with family, friends and colleagues. There may however be some points that are not applicable to every type of relationship.

John Gottman's Four Horsemen are:

1. Criticism

2. Contempt

3. Defensiveness

4. Stonewalling

Criticism can be a common problem in relationships, and leads to other more harmful behaviours. What starts as a complaint can turn into criticism and then to contempt.

Contempt is a sense of superiority over the other person (which can be seen in sarcastic comments, for example) and is often fuelled by long-term negative thoughts about the other person.

Defensiveness is actually a way of blaming the other person and implying the problem is them.

Stonewalling is a way of avoiding an argument, but really it avoids the relationship as a whole. It is a way of disengaging emotionally from the relationship.

All of these can be counteracted by practising the happiness skills of positivity, gratitude, non-judgement, mindfulness, awareness of strengths, hope, meaning and motivation. These skills can help us build a positive, mindful, emotionally intelligent relationship. If we practise compassion toward ourselves and the other, it will help us to begin to understand what is really causing the initial problem, and we will be less inclined to criticize. It will also help us be more receptive to repair attempts too.

Some of the aspects that Gottman says support a good relationship are:

- Strong friendship and trust (heart of the relationship)
- Being intimately familiar with each other's life
- Making a habit of staying deeply connected (especially through life's changes)
- The joy of feeling known and understood (ask detailed, open-ended questions)
- Nurturing fondness, admiration and respect
- Being aware of and acknowledging the other's positive qualities
- Having shared meaning, values and goals
- Having shared experiences and memories

Staying connected with small and regular bits of communication is important – for example, talk over dinner (turn off all devices) or go for walks together. Make sure you are listening actively and are fully engaged in the conversation, empathizing with and validating each other's emotions. Hearing and respecting each other's feelings and opinions will ensure you both feel understood and connected.

Gottman also talks about "bids", which are when we seek things such as affection, support or connection. They can be small or large, like a hug or helping with an elderly relative. When someone responds positively toward you when you make a bid it will build trust and connection.

Life is made up of the small moments, and these small moments accumulate to much more than a big annual holiday, for example. You always have a choice when you know your partner needs a bit of help or is struggling – you can choose to turn toward them and offer help or you can choose to turn away and pretend you were unaware.

Each time you respond positively to a bid you put a deposit into your relationship "current account". This will improve your relationship in the present moment, but some of that deposit will also go into the relationship "savings account". The "savings account" is important when the relationship goes through hard times, which is a natural thing for all relationships. If the other person has a good amount accumulated in the savings account, then the relationship will be more resilient, as you will draw on those things from the savings account to help you work through the difficulties. However, if there is little to nothing in the account, then you are more liable to walk away sooner.

BUILDING TRUST

Brené Brown researched a similar concept, which involves building trust over time in relationships through each trustworthy action. It's helpful to understand the different component parts of trust, so she created the acronym BRAVING to explain, as follows:

- **Boundaries** – respect each other's boundaries and be willing to say "No".

- **Reliability** – do what you say you'll do.

- **Accountability** – own your own mistakes, apologize and make amends.

- **Vault** – make sure confidences are kept.

- **Integrity** – choose to do what is right; courage over comfort.

- **Non-judgement** – enables the ability to talk honestly and make bids without the fear of judgement.

- **Generosity** – apply the most generous interpretation of other people's intentions, words and actions.

The more trust and connection, the better the relationship. And if it's a romantic relationship then your sex life will improve too.

The Power of Touch

The skin is the body's largest organ, so it's no surprise that we can be significantly affected by touch (or lack of it). There has been a lot of research into the positive effects (on a physical and psychological level) of touch, whether that's giving it or receiving it. Think of how much regular physical contact you are having. Are you tactile with your friends and family? Do you occasionally touch people on the arm when you are talking to them? Are you a hugger? Are you physically close with your partner? Do you go for massages? Going for a massage can be a great way to reconnect with your body, enhance your wellbeing and reduce your stress levels all at the same time.

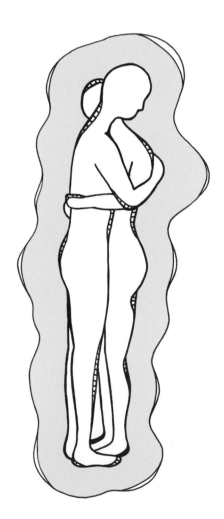

Cultures that are more tactile toward their children are generally found to have less adult violence. One study compared adolescents interacting with their friends in fast-food restaurants in Paris and in Miami. It revealed that the French adolescents were more tactile with each other compared to their American counterparts. The Americans did more self-soothing (touching their own hair and rubbing their arms, for example), while the French were less verbally and physically aggressive.

There is evidence that self-soothing behaviours have similar calming effects to physical affection with another person (such as lowering the heart rate and reducing the stress hormone cortisol), but it's not as effective as directly receiving or giving touch.

Research shows that when people have contact with their partner before a stressful event, it lowers their blood pressure. Affectionate physical contact, for example holding hands and hugging, will lower reactivity to stressful life events and could even help improve cardiovascular health.

Relationship satisfaction is closely linked to physical affection and couples or family members who are in a good relationship will be more affectionate with each other. An important point is how you respond when your partner touches you, strong reciprocity is a good indicator of emotional intimacy and satisfaction. Happy relationships ideally have a balance between what we are doing for the other person and what we are receiving from them.

Three Degrees...of Influence

Research on "emotional contagion" has shown that we can have an effect on our friend, our friend's friend and our friend's friend's friend. Even though you may never know that third person, you can influence them in a positive or negative way.

This was realized by the researchers James Fowler and Nicholas Christakis. Fowler said, "Even people we don't know and have never met have a bigger effect on our mood than substantial increases in income." Their research showed that a happy neighbour increases your happiness by 34 per cent, while a friend who lives within a mile increases it by 42 per cent.

We all need to be mindful of the effect we are having on others and that others are having on us. How wonderful to know that if you increase your happiness you will not only improve your own life but you can have a positive effect on multiple people, some you know and others you'll never know.

The Top Benefits of Good Relationships

Improving your relationships will result in:

- Improved physical health
- Improved mental health (becoming less depressed and anxious)
- Improved happiness
- Improved life satisfaction
- Improved optimism
- Improved positive affect
- Increased reciprocity
- Increased trust (deepens and strengthens relationships)
- Longevity
- Better memory function
- Less mental deterioration
- Fewer negative emotions
- Less negative rumination
- Lower blood pressure
- Less stress

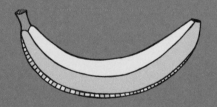

Final Points

Before I close, there are just a few final things I would like to say. I have deliberately not included the importance to our wellbeing of eating healthy food, getting enough exercise and sleep, avoiding drugs and not consuming too much alcohol. Aside from the fact that I'm a Positive Psychologist rather than an expert in any of those subjects, there are plenty of books and information online, which offer all the proper guidance and expertise you need.

However, I will say all those things are extremely important for our wellbeing. Because we are a complete system, we can't focus on just one aspect, while neglecting another and expecting the whole system to function at its best. For example, lack of sleep interferes with brain growth and neuroplasticity. Learning and memory also happen during sleep, as information is transferred from short-term to long-term memory. If you feel sleep-deprived then a nap in the afternoon is a great way to recover a bit of sleep, plus it can boost and restore brainpower.

I believe that happier people make healthier choices. So the more you increase your happiness and life satisfaction, the more likely you are to take care of yourself on every level – psychologically, physically and spiritually.

My intention and hope is that this book will help people grow their own happiness and maintain a good level of life satisfaction. It can also be used as a preventative method to help prevent mental health issues arising or reoccurring. In my psychotherapeutic work, I often help people when they fear that their mental health issues, such as depression, will reoccur. Fear feeds on itself, so when someone is scared of something, that fear can increase. The way to let go and feel empowered is to deepen your understanding, such as knowing what your triggers are and what the signs are. Also what things you can do to improve a situation and help you feel in control.

People are triggered into a positive or negative mental state in a variety of ways – the key is to know yourself well enough that you know what your triggers are. If a person had alcoholic parents, for example, they could be triggered if, on a rare occasion, their partner comes home drunk.

It may be that you are able to anticipate the trigger and do something to avert it. If you do become triggered, ideally you will recognize it and what has caused it, allowing you to dissipate the emotion yourself, without it having a negative effect on you or those around you.

RECOGNIZING THE SIGNS

Most of the time there are several signs that a mental health issue is arising. It is common for clients to come to me saying they were "hit" with depression, that it came "out of the blue", and they "didn't see it coming". However, once we start reflecting on the months, or even years, leading up to the depression, they are then able to see the signs and issues that needed to be addressed. The more mindful you are toward yourself, the more you will notice the signs. Naturally, it is easier to make a minor adjustment than to wait until a major adjustment needs to be made.

Those minor adjustments can be made using the various exercises in this book, and empowerment comes from knowing you have techniques that will work for you. I wanted to make the book and exercises within it as inclusive as possible. The intention is they are suitable for everyone, irrespective of age, gender, financial situation or psychological and physical abilities.

There are many ways to positively affect your happiness, as well as that of those around you, and hopefully you will realize that you have more choice and control over your wellbeing than you may have known before reading this book.

TO PRACTISE OR NOT?

If you choose not to practise any of the exercises in the book, then it could be because you think you don't need to. I remember one person saying to me, "If I increased my happiness by 40 per cent I'd burst!" I thought this was amazing. However, aside from that one person, everyone else I've met has always said they would benefit from increasing their happiness. So, if you do choose not to do the exercises, I invite you to look deeply within yourself and ask yourself why you are making that choice. Are there any blocks that could be lifted to clear a path toward your right to happiness?

"Never underestimate the power of planting a seed."

Stress Testing

We all know stress is bad for us – but how bad is bad? There is a big difference between acute stress and chronic stress.

Acute stress happens when we are triggered in the present moment, for example, if we are speaking in public or encountering a dangerous animal. In this type of situation, stress levels will rise sharply, enabling us to respond appropriately to the situation (give a great talk or run away). After the event, stress levels return to normal. Acute stress can be beneficial in that it enables us to react in a way that might not happen if we didn't have that response.

Chronic stress, however, is harmful. It has a negative effect on the brain and body and occurs when a person feels stressed for long periods of time. These bouts have sadly become a common feature of everyday life – not only is stress seen as a primary cause of illness, it is estimated that between 60 and 90 per cent of visits to doctors are due to stress-related illness.

According to research, these are just a few things of the things that stress can cause:

• Impaired learning

• Impaired memory

• Contribution to symptoms of depression and other mental health issues

• Contribution to sleep problems

• Reduction of sexual activity and satisfaction

• A decrease in relationship satisfaction

• Higher likelihood of alcohol and drug addiction/relapse

• Higher levels of aggression

• Inflammatory bowel disease, irritable bowel syndrome

• Coronary heart disease

EPIGENETICS ALL AROUND

Epigenetics is the study of the external changes that affect gene activity and expression within our cells. These outside changes can be things such as our environment (whether it is clean or polluted), what we consume (food, alcohol, drugs), and how we think (anxious or relaxed). These are just some of the things that can affect gene activity. For example, if we perceive the world as threatening then we will produce stress hormones and inflammatory agents. In an experiment where these hormones and agents were added to cells in a petri dish, they were shown to stop some cells growing, potentially killing them off. This is why the cell biologist Bruce Lipton claims that chronic stress is the primary cause of illness.

Think Small

The way we think has such a powerful effect that it can be seen on a cellular level. The mind interprets our perceptions and our brains then produce the chemicals accordingly. It is up to us to be mindful of whether we are likely to be producing neurochemicals that are helpful or harmful to us.

First, there is perception – we perceive whatever we are seeing, hearing, smelling, tasting and feeling.

Second, there is interpretation – we interpret the perception according to our intuition and past experiences.

Third, neurochemicals are released – the interpretation dictates what, if any, neurochemicals are released. Neurochemicals are released into the blood, which affects cell behaviour.

GOOD AND BAD CHEMICALS

There are many ways in which we can release the neurochemicals that are good for us. For example, as we saw in the Positivity chapter (see page 86), there is the opportunity for two releases of dopamine simply by listening to music. Research also shows that looking at photos of someone you love will light up the dopamine circuits of the brain (see the exercise on page 98).

Oxytocin is known as the hugging hormone, and studies have shown the link between hugs and oxytocin. As discussed in the chapter on Relationships (page 178), hugs and physical contact with a trusted person are important for our wellbeing in many ways – the release of the feel-good neurochemical oxytocin being one of them.

Similarly, there are different ways in which you can reduce harmful brain chemicals, such as the stress hormone cortisol. One study showed how children's cortisol levels could be reduced after a phone call with their mother. They found all the children had a similar lowering of cortisol levels and increase in oxytocin levels, whether they were with their mothers in person or speaking to them over the phone. Obviously they had to have a good relationship with their mother in order for this to happen.

Practising mindfulness also reduces cortisol levels. The point is, the choices you make in terms of your behaviour and the way you think will have a profound effect on you – it would be a mistake to underestimate this.

When we criticize ourselves, it is perceived by our brain as a threat – this is because the amygdala (the part of the brain involved in the fight or flight response) is triggered. The amygdala is in the old part of the brain and is designed to react instantly to threats. However, it cannot tell the difference between a physical threat and a psychological threat, nor does it distinguish between an actual threat and a perceived threat.

When the amygdala is triggered, adrenaline and cortisol are released to enable fight or flight. Obviously, this is great if you do need to fight or run, but not so great if you don't. When we criticize ourselves, we fill the body with adrenaline and cortisol, in other words we are the attacker and the attacked. Eventually, there will be a cortisol overload, which will result in the body shutting down in order to cope and this can show itself as depression and/or anxiety. You need to be aware of whether you are attacking yourself, or helping and supporting yourself. All the techniques in this book enable you to aid your own wellbeing and happiness.

Feelings of warmth and compassion deactivate the body's threat system and activate the attachment system, calming the amygdala and producing oxytocin. Oxytocin lessens the tendency for the mind to attach to negative information.

We must remember to be our own caregiver (by practising self-compassion, for instance). We need to create oxytocin to reduce cortisol and make ourselves feel safe, comforted and able to cope with whatever situation we are in.

Two-way System

Most human beings have a two-way system, where the body affects the mind and the mind affects the body. The social psychologist Amy Cuddy has done a TED talk on power poses (called *Your Body Language May Shape Who You Are*) and it's one of the most popular TED talks to date. In it, she discusses her research into the effects of body language. She found that adopting a "power pose" for two minutes can make you feel more powerful and confident. Participants had a 20 per cent increase in testosterone and a 25 per cent decrease in cortisol if they adopted a "high power pose" (standing straight, hands on hips, elbows out, chin up and feet apart).

The main point about a high power pose is adopting body language that is open and takes up space. Low power poses involve making ourselves small and closed off (legs and arms crossed, not standing straight and keeping our heads slightly down). Be mindful of your body – are you sitting or standing in a powerless or powerful way? Are you empowering or disempowering yourself? You can use these power poses to give yourself a boost before a stressful situation, such as a job interview.

The Great Outdoors

Finally, I want to talk about the power of nature. The evidence for the positive effects of nature is indisputable. Walking in nature, or even just looking at a picture of nature, significantly improves our cognitive performance, compared to a walking in a city environment.

One study showed the positive effects of walking in nature for people who have a major depressive disorder. Patients who have had surgery recover better when they have a view of nature out of their hospital window, compared to a view of a brick wall, for instance. They leave hospital sooner, have fewer complications and need less pain relief. In the workplace, a view of nature can have a significantly positive effect on stress and job satisfaction.

Research shows that self-esteem and mood can be improved by exercising in nature. This positive effect can be further enhanced by the presence of water, such as a river or lake. People who have had mental health issues show the greatest improvements in their self-esteem.

We know now that people are spending more time indoors and interacting with technology. There even appears to be an increase in short-sightedness in children and adolescents, and research has shown that spending time outside reduces the risk of this. Being in nature replenishes our attention. Research has found that certain creative and problem-solving tasks can be improved by 50 per cent after a four-day retreat in nature away from technology.

Forest bathing or forest therapy – simply the art of immersing oneself in nature – is widely practised in Japan. Research reveals that the positive effects of time spent in a forest environment (decreased cortisol levels, decreased sympathetic nervous system activity, decreased blood pressure and decreased heart rate) continued for weeks after people returned to their normal urban life. In other words, people feel calmer and more relaxed for up to a month after time spent walking and being in a beautiful forest.

Don't worry if you don't have access to a forest, as any contact with nature will be beneficial. Even having a plant in your room or pictures of nature on your walls will have a positive impact. It's a great idea to have a beautiful picture of a forest or a beach (or whatever creates a sense of awe within you) as the screensaver on your computer screen. If you live in a particularly urban environment, challenge yourself to notice as many bits of nature as you can when you go out. We can all look up at the sky – a blue sky is amazing, clouds are mesmerizing, stars are magical.

The beauty of nature is all around us, it is up to us to stop and take notice. The more you do this, the more you will feel a sense of awe at a little weed which manages to survive in a sea of concrete and pollution. Nature is truly amazing and always inspiring and has the power to truly enhance our wellbeing and happiness.

I hope you feel empowered by everything you have read in this book, knowing that there are multiple things you can do to grow your own happiness, knowing there are simple but effective techniques, some of which will give you instant results and some of which can be mastered over time. The power, my friend, is in your hands.

Resources

Guided meditation

Visit my website at www.growyourownhappiness.com or search for "Deborah Smith meditation" on YouTube to find some guided mindfulness meditations, including Compassion Meditation. I've included different lengths of guided meditations, from two to twenty minutes.

Recommended organizations

Here are some of my recommended organizations that will be able to support you as you grow your own happiness:

• Samaritans – www.samaritans.org

• Action For Happiness – www.actionforhappiness.org

• London Buddhist Vihara – www.londonbuddhistvihara.org

• The Rahula Trust – www.rahula-trust.org

Volunteering

Here are some great websites for finding voluntary work, where you can get involved and meet like-minded people. These are just some ideas and starting points to help you find something that is right for you:

• Do it org – do-it.org

• 2 minute beach clean – www.beachclean.net

• Surfers Against Sewage – www.sas.org.uk

• Marine Conservation Society – www.mcsuk.org

• The Woodland Trust – www.woodlandtrust.org.uk

• UK National Council For Voluntary Organisations – www.ncvo.org.uk

• UK National Association for Voluntary and Community Action – www.navca.org.uk

• Voluntary Service Overseas – www.vsointernational.org

• United Nations Volunteers - https://www.unv.org/

References

INTRODUCTION

13 *One of the founders*   Seligman, M. (2002) *Authentic Happiness: Using the New Positive Psychology to Realize your Potential for Lasting Fulfillment.* New York: Free Press

16 *Through extensive research*   Lyubomirsky, S., Sheldon, K.M. & Schkade, D. (2005) Pursuing happiness: The architecture of sustainable change. *Review of General Psychology*, 9 (2)

21 *Our power of visualization*   Pascual-Leone, A., Dang, N., Cohen, L., Brasil-Neto, J., Cammarota, A. & Hallett, M. (1995) Modulation of muscle response evoked by transcranial magnetic stimulation during the acquisition of new fine motor skills. *Journal of Neurophysiology* vol.74: no.3

33 *Your physical health*   Davidson, K., Mostofsky, E. & Whang, W. (2010) Don't worry, be happy: positive affect and reduced 10-year incident coronary heart disease: The Canadian Nova Scotia Health Survey. *European Heart Journal*, 31 (9): 1065–1070

33 *Your physical health*   Bhattacharyya, M.R., Whitehead, D.L., Rakhit, R., Steptoe, A. (2008) Depressed mood, positive affect, and heart rate variability in patients with suspected coronary artery disease. *Psychosom Medicine* vol.70: 1020–7

33 *Your physical health*   Cohen, S., Doyle, W.J., Turner, R.B., Alper, C.M. & Skoner, D.P. (2003) Emotional style and susceptibility to the common cold. *Psychosom Medicine* vol.65: 652–7

33 *Your physical health*   Steptoe, A. & Wardle, J. (2005) Positive affect and biological function in everyday life. *Neurobiology of aging* vol.26: 108–112

33 *Your mental health*   Papousek, I., Nauschnegg, K., Paechter, M., Lackner, H., Goswami, N. & Schulter, G. (2010) Trait and state positive affect and cardiovascular recovery from experimental academic stress. *Biological Psychology* vol. 83: 108–115

33 *Your mental health*   Lyubomirsky, S., King, L. & Diener, E. (2005) The benefits of frequent positive affect: does happiness lead to success? *Psychological Bulletin* vol.131: 803–855

33 *Your relationships with*   Berkman, L. (1984) Assessing the physical health effects of social networks and social support. *Annual Reviews* 5:413–32

33 *Your relationships with*   Emmons, R.A., & Shelton, C.M. (2002) Gratitude and the science of positive psychology. *Handbook of Positive Psychology.* Oxford: Oxford University Press

33 *Your performance at work*   Oswald, A., Proto, E. & Sgroi, D. (2015) Happiness and productivity. *Journal of Labour Economics* vol.33. 4

33 *Your performance at work*   Lyubomirsky, S., King, L. & Diener, E. (2005) The benefits of frequent positive affect: Does happiness lead to success? *Psychological Bulletin*, 131, 803–855

CHAPTER 1: GRATITUDE

44 *We are also*   Bartlett, M. & De Steno, D. (2006) Gratitude and prosocial behaviour: Helping when it costs you. *Psychological Science* vol.17: 319–325

44 *Yet again it's a win-win situation*   Thoits, P. & Hewitt, L. (2001) Volunteer work and well-being. *Journal of Health and Social Behavior* vol.42: 115–131

44 *Decades of research*   Trivers, R. (1971) The evolution of reciprocal altruism. *Quarterly Review of Biology* vol.46: 35–57

44 *Decades of research*   McCullough, M., Emmons, R. & Tsang, J. (2002) The grateful disposition: A conceptual and empirical topography. *Journal of Personality and Social Psychology* vol.82: 112–127

46 *Research into the effects*   Emmons, R. & McCullough, M., (2003) Counting blessings versus burdens: An experimental investigation of gratitude and subjective wellbeing in daily life. *Journal of Personality and Social Psychology* vol.84: 377–389

46 *There is a difference*   McCraty, R., Atkinson, W., Tiller, G., Rein, G. & Watkins, A. (1995) The effects of emotions on short-term power spectrum analysis of heart rate variability. *American Journal of Cardiology* vol.76: 1089–1092

49 *Take this test*   Emmons, R. & McCullough, M., (2003) Counting blessings versus burdens: An experimental investigation of gratitude and subjective wellbeing in daily life. *Journal of Personality and Social Psychology* vol.84: 377–389

CHAPTER 2: MINDFULNESS

59 *In its contemporary sense* Kabat-Zinn, J. (1994) *Wherever You Go, There You Are: Mindfulness Meditation In Everyday Life.* New York: Hyperion

60 *Stronger immune system; Decreased blood pressure; Reduced anxiety* Carlson, L., Speca, M., Faris, P. & Patel, K. (2007) One year pre–post intervention follow-up of psychological, immune, endocrine and blood pressure outcomes of mindfulness-based stress reduction (MBSR) in breast and prostate cancer outpatients. *Brain Behaviour Immunity* vol.21: 1038–1049

60 *Reduced anxiety* Hofmann, S., Sawyer, A., Witt, A. & Oh, D. (2010) The effect of mindfulness-based therapy on anxiety and depression: a meta-analytic review. *Journal of Consulting and Clinical Psychology* vol.78: 169–183

60 *Reduced stress and substance abuse* Brewer, J., Sinha, R., Chen, J., Michalsen, R., Babuscio, T., Nich, C. & Rounsaville, B. (2009) Mindfulness training and stress reactivity in substance abuse: Results from a randomized, controlled stage I pilot study. *Substance Abuse: Official Publication of the Association for Medical Education and Research in Substance Abuse* vol.30: 306–317

60 *Increased positive emotions* Fredrickson, B., Cohn, M., Coffey, K., Pek, J. & Finkel, S. (2008) Open hearts build lives: Positive emotions, induced through loving-kindness meditation, build consequential personal resources. *Journal of Personality and Social Psychology* vol.95: 1045–1062

60 *Decreased rumination* Campbell, T., Labelle, L., Bacon, S., Faris, P. & Carlson, L. (2012) Impact of mindfulness-based stress reduction (MBSR) on attention, rumination and resting blood pressure in women with cancer: A waitlist-controlled study. *Journal of Behavioural Medicine* vol.35: 262–271

60 *Increased concentration* Bostanov, V., Keune, P., Kotchoubey, B. & Hautzinger, M. (2012) Event-related brain potentials reflect increased concentration ability after mindfulness-based cognitive therapy for depression: A randomized clinical trial. *Psychiatry Research* vol.99: iss.3

60 *Increased memory and cognitive function* Mrazek, M., Franklin, M., Phillips, D., Baird, B. & Schooler, J. (2013) Mindfulness training improves working memory capacity and performance while reducing mind wandering. *Psychological Science* vol.24: 776–781

61 *Research undertaken* Holzel, B. *et al* (2011) Mindfulness practice leads to increases in regional brain grey matter density. *Psychiatry Resources* vol.191: 36–43

61 *These are all crucial factors* Killingsworth, M. & Gilbert, D. (2010) A wandering mind is an unhappy mind. *Science* vol.330: 932

62 *We used to think that* Draganski, B., Gaser, C., Kempermann, G., Kuhn, G., Winkler, J., Buchel, C. & May, A. (2006) Temporal and spatial dynamics of brain structure changes during extensive learning. *The Journal of Neuroscience* vol.26: 6314–6317

62 *The amygdala is a key part* Hozel, B., Carmody, J., Evans, K., Hoge, E., Dusek, J., Morgan, L., Pitman, R. & Lazar, S. (2010) Stress reduction correlates with structural changes in the amygdala. *Social Cognitive and Affective Neuroscience* vol.5: 11–17

70 *Research shows that* Hutcherson, A., Seppala, E. and Gross, J. (2008) Loving kindness meditation increases social connectedness. *Emotion, American Psychological Association* vol.8: 720–724

CHAPTER 3: POSITIVITY

87 *Barbara Fredrickson* Fredrickson, B. L. (2001) The role of positive emotions in positive psychology: The broaden-and-build theory of positive emotions. *American Psychologist* vol.56: 218–226

88 *Our brains are more attuned* Ito, T.A., Larsen, J.T., Smith, N.K. & Cacioppo, J.T. (1998) Negative information weighs more heavily on the brain: The negativity bias in evaluative categorizations. *Journal of Personality and Social Psychology* vol.75: 887–900

90 *Laughter makes us more positive* Bains, G.S., Berk, L.S., Daher, N., Lohman, E., Schwab, E., Petrofsky, J. & Deshpande, P. (2014) The effect of humor on short-term memory in older adults: a new component for whole-person wellness. *Advanced Mind Body Medicine* vol.28: 16–24

90 *According to Rod Martin* Martin, R., Puhlik-Doris, P., Larsen, G., Gray, J. & Weir, K. (2003) Individual differences in uses of humour and their relation to psychological well-being: Development of the Humour Styles Questionnaire. *Journal of Research in Personality* vol.37: 48–75

92 *Smile! – the very act of* Kraft, T. & Pressman, S. (2012) Grin and bear it: The influence of manipulated facial expression on the stress response. *Psychological Science* vol.23: 1372

93 *Research has shown* Lewis, M. & Bowler, P. (2009) Botulinum toxin cosmetic therapy correlates with a more positive mood. *Journal of Cosmetic Dermatology* vol.8: 24–26

94 *Studies have shown* Fredrickson, B.L. (2013) Updated thinking on positivity ratios. *American Psychologist* vol.68: 814–822

99 *Dopamime – a mood-enhancing* Salimpoor, V., Benovoy, M., Larcher, K., Dagher, A. & Zatorre, R. (2011) Anatomically distinct dopamine release during anticipation and experience of peak emotion to music. *Nature Neuroscience* vol.14: 257–262

100 *Similarly, if you end a stressful day* Savage, B., Lujan, H., Thipparthi, R. & DiCarlo, S. (2017) Humour, laughter, learning and health! A brief review. *Advances in Physiology Education* vol.31: 341–347

100 *Remember that humour* Hassed, C. (2001) How humour keeps you well. *Australian Family Physician* vol.30: 25–28

CHAPTER 4: RESILIENCE

103 *As discussed in* Wilson, T. & Gilbert, D. (2013) The impact bias is alive and well. *Journal of Personality and Social Psychology* vol.105: 740–748

107 *The research shows* Peterson, C. & Barrett, L. (1987) Explanatory style and academic performance among university freshman. *Journal of Personality and Social Psychology* vol.53: 603–607

107 *The research shows* Scheier, M.F., Matthews, K.A., Owens, J.F., Magovern, G.J., Lefebvre, R.C., Abbott, R.A. & Carver, C.S. (1989) Dispositional optimism and recovery from coronary artery bypass surgery: The beneficial effects on physical and psychological well-being. *Journal of Personality and Social Psychology* vol.57: 1024–1040

111 *Post Traumatic Growth Test* Tedeschi, R. & Calhoun, L. (1996) The post traumatic growth inventory: Measuring the positive legacy of trauma. *Journal of Traumatic Stress* vol.9: 455–471

115 *It doesn't matter* Joseph, S. & Linley, P.A. (2005) Positive adjustment to threatening events: An organismic valuing theory of growth through adversity. *Review of General Psychology* vol.9: 262–280

115 *It doesn't matter* Linley, A. & Joseph, S. (2004) Positive change following trauma and adversity: A review. *Journal of Traumatic Stress* vol.17: 11–21

117 *Research shows that* see 111

CHAPTER 5: AWARENESS OF STRENGTHS

123 *However, according to research* Hill, J. (2001) How well do we know our strengths? Paper presented at the British Psychological Society Centenary Conference (April), Glasgow, Scotland

123 *Research conducted by Gallup* The Gallup Poll: Public Opinion (2012) Rowman & Littlefield

124 *These virtues stand up* McGrath, R. (2014) Character strengths in 75 nations: An update. *The Journal of Positive Psychology* vol.10: 41–52

125 *The list on the following pages* © Copyright 2004–2018, VIA Institute on Character. All Rights Reserved. Used with permission. www.viacharacter.org

132 *Research shows greater satisfaction* Kashdan, T., Blalock, D., Young, K., Machell, K., Monfort, S., Mcknight, P. & Ferssizidis, P. (2017) Personality strengths in romantic relationships: Measuring perceptions of benefits and costs and their impact on personal and relational well-being. *Psychological Assessment* vol.30: 241–258

133 *Research indicates that social anxiety* Freidlin, P., Littman-Ovadia, H. & Niemiec, R. (2017) Positive psychopathology: Social anxiety via character strengths underuse and overuse. *Personality and Individual Difference* vol.108: 50–54

135 *Interestingly, research shows* McNulty, J.K. (2011). The dark side of forgiveness: The tendency to forgive predicts continued psychological and physical aggression in marriage. *Personality & Social Psychology Bulletin* vol.37: 770–783

CHAPTER 6: HOPE

143 *He defines hope as* Lopez, S. (2013) *Making Hope Happen*. Atria Books

146 *The Schools of Hope* The Rahula Trust: http://www.rahula-trust.org

160 *One study, conducted in 2007* Berg, C., Rapoff, M., Snyder, C. & Belmont, J. (2007) The relationship of children's hope to pediatric asthma treatment adherence. *The Journal of Positive Psychology* 176–184

161 *Greater success* Snyder, C.R. (1994). *The Psychology of Hope: You Can Get There From Here*. New York: Free Press

161 *Improves academic performance* Snyder, C.R., Shorey, H.S., Cheavens, J., Pulvers, K.M., Adams, V.H. & Wiklund, C. (2002) Hope and academic success in college. *Journal of Educational Psychology* vol.94: 820–826; *see also* 143

161 *Predicts grades* Snyder, C.R., Harris, C., Anderson, J.R., Holleran, S.A., Irving, L.M., Sigmon, S.T., Yoshinobu, L., Gibb, J., Langelle, C. & Harney, P. (1991) The will and the ways: Development and validation of an individual-differences measure of hope. *Journal of Personality and Social Psychology* vol.60: 540–585; ; *see also* 143

161 *Predicts grades*   Ciarrochi, J., Heaven, P. & Davies, F. (2007) The impact of hope, self-esteem, and attributional style on adolescents' school grades and emotional well-being: A longitudinal study. *Journal of Research in Personality* vol.41: 1161–1178

161 *Predicts ongoing enrolment; workplace productivity; absenteeism; increases happiness; see* 143

161 *Predicts athletic outcomes*   Curry, L.A., Snyder, C.R., Cook, D.L., Ruby, B.C. & Rehm, M. (1997) Role of hope in academic and sport achievement. Journal of Personality and Social Psychology vol.73: 1257–1267

161 *Increases tolerance to pain*   Snyder, C., Ber. C., Woodward, J., Gum, A., Rand, K., Wrobleski, K., Brown, J. & Hackman, A. (2005) Hope against the cold: Individual differences in trait hope and acute pain tolerance on the cold pressor task. Journal of Personality vol.73: 287–312; *see also* 143

161 *Reduces depression*   Cheavens, J.S., Feldman, D.B., Gum, A., Michael, S.T. & Snyder, C.R. (2006) Hope theory in a community sample: A pilot investigation. Social Indicators Research vol.77: 61–78

CHAPTER 7: MEANING & MOTIVATION

168 *The meaning and motivation*   Frankl, V. (1959) *Man's Search for Meaning: An Introduction to Logotherapy*, Boston: Beacon

170 *Being clear about your M&Ms*   Cotton Bronk, K., Hill, P., Lapsley, D., Talib, T. & Finch, H. (2009) Purpose, hope, and life satisfaction in three age groups. *The Journal of Positive Psychology* vol.4: 500–510

175 *She concluded*   Duckworth, A. (2016) *The Power of Passion and Perseverance*, Penguin Random House

176 *However, when people are close*   Society for Consumer Psychology (2017, April 3) The secret to staying motivated. *Science Daily* (retrieved August 1, 2018 from www.sciencedaily.com/releases/2017/04/170403151140.htm)

177 *The top benefits of*   Park, N., Park, M. & Peterson, C. (2010) When is the search for meaning related to life satisfaction? *Applied Psychology: Health and Wellbeing* vol.2: 1–13; *see also* 168

CHAPTER 8: RELATIONSHIPS

181 *Research shows that*   Shapiro, S., Brown, K. & Biegel, G. (2007) Teaching self-care to caregivers: Effects of mindfulness-based stress reduction on mental health of therapists in training. *Training and education in professional psychology* vol.1: no.2

182 *Self-compassion is recognized*   Neff, K.D. (2009) Self-compassion. In M.R. Leary & R.H. Hoyle (Eds.) *Handbook of Individual Differences in Social Behaviour* (561–573) New York: Guilford Press

182 *Self-compassion also helps lessen*   Neff., K.D, Rude, S. & Kirkpatrick, K. (2007) An examination of self-compassion in relation to positive psychological functioning and personality traits. *Journal of Research in Personality* vol.41: 908–916

186 This exercise was adapted from the Self-compassion Break by Kristin Neff

186 *Kristin Neff's Self-compassion scale*   Raes, F., Pommier, E., Neff, K.D. & Van Gucht, D. (2011) Construction and factorial validation of a short form of the Self-Compassion Scale. *Clinical Psychology & Psychotherapy* vol.18: 250–255

191 *Research shows that self-esteem*   Neff, K.D & Vonk, R. (2009) Self-compassion versus global self-esteem: Two different ways of relating to oneself. *Journal of Personality* vol.77: no.1

196 *Although Gottman's research*   Gottman, J. & Silver, N. (2015) *The Seven Principles for Making Marriage Work*. Orion Publishing Group

199 *It is helpful to understand*   Brown, B. (2015) *Rising Strong: If We're Brave Enough, Often Enough, We Will Fall*. Vermilion, Penguin Random House

200 *Going for a massage*   Field, T. (2010) Touch for socioemotional and physical well-being: A review. *Developmental Review* vol.30: 367–383

201 *Cultures that are*   Field, T. (1999) American adolescents touch each other less and are more aggressive toward their peers as compared with French adolescents. *Adolescence* vol.34: 753–758

201 *Research shows that when people*   Grewen, K., Anderson, B., Girdler, S. & Light, K. (2003) Warm partner contact is related to lower cardiovascular reactivity. *Behavioural Medicine* vol.29: 123–130

202 *This was realized by the researchers*   Fowler, J. & Christakis, N. (2008) Dynamic spread of happiness in a large social network: Longitudinal analysis over 20 years in the Framingham Heart Study. *BMJ*

FINAL POINTS

210 *These bouts have sadly*   Perkins, A., (1994) Saving money by reducing stress. *Harvard Business Review*, 72 (6): 12

210 *Impaired learning; Impaired memory;*   Bowman, R., Beck, K. & Luinea, V. (2002) Chronic stress effects on memory: Sex differences in performance and monoaminergic activity. *Neuroscience and Biobehavioural Reviews* vol.5: no.2

210 *Contribution to symptoms of depression* Hammen, C. (2005) Stress and depression. *Annual Review of Clinical Psychology* vol.1: 293–319

210 *Contribution to sleep problems* Åkerstedt, T. (2006) Psychosocial stress and impaired sleep. *Scandinavian Journal of Work, Environment & Health* vol.32: 493–501

210 *Reduction of sexual activity; Decrease in relationship satisfaction* Bodenmann G., Atkins D.C., Schär M. & Poffet V. (2010) The association between daily stress and sexual activity. *Journal of Family Psychology* vol.24: 271–279

210 *Higher likelihood of alcohol* Sinha, R., (2008) Chronic stress, drug use and vulnerability to addiction. *Annals of the New York Academy of Sciences* 1141

210 *Higher levels of aggression* Kruk, M.R., Halász, J., Meelis, W. & Haller, J. (2004) Fast positive feedback between the adrenocortical stress response and a brain mechanism involved in aggressive behaviour. *Behavioural Neuroscience* vol.118: 1062–1070

210 *Inflammatory bowel disease* Konturek, P.C., Brzozowski, T. & Konturek, S.J. (2011) Stress and the gut: Pathophysiology, clinical consequences, diagnostic approach and treatment options. *Journal of Physiology and Pharmacology* vol.62: 591–599

210 *Coronary heart disease* Steptoe, A. & Kivimaki, M. (2012) Stress and cardiovascular disease. *Nature Reviews Cardiology* vol.9: 360–370

211 *In an experiment* Lipton, B. (2013) *The Honeymoon Effect.* Hay House

213 *Research also shows* Bartels, A. & Zeki, S. (2000) The Neural Basis of Romantic Love. *Neuroreport* vol.11: no.17

213 *Oxytocin is known* Light, K., Grewen, K. & Amico, J. (2005) More frequent partner hugs and higher oxytocin levels are linked to lower blood pressure and heart rate in premenopausal women. *Biology Psychology* vol.69: no.1

213 *They found all the* Seltzer, L., Ziegler, T. & Pollak, S. (2010) Social vocalizations can release oxytocin in humans. *Proceedings of the Royal Society* B, 1098

214 *When we criticize ourselves* Neff, K. (2011) *Self Compassion. Stop Beating Yourself Up and Leave Insecurity Behind.* Hodder & Stoughton

214 *Feelings of warmth* Harmer, C. (2009) Oxytocin enhances processing of positive versus negative emotional information in healthy male volunteers. *Journal of Psychopharmacology*, 241–248

215 *The social psychologist* Carney, D., Cuddy, A. & Yap, A. (2010) Power posing: Brief nonverbal displays affect neuroendocrine levels and risk tolerance. *Psychological Science* vol.21: 1363–1368

216 *Walking in nature* Berman, M., Jonides, J. & Kaplan, S. (2008) The cognitive benefits of interacting with nature. *Psychological Science* vol.19: 1207–1212

216 *One study showed* Berman, M., Kross, E., Krpan, K., Askren, M., Burson, A., Deldin, Kaplan, S., Sherdell, L., Gotlib, I. & Jonides, J. (2012) Interacting with nature improves cognition and affect for individuals with depression. *Journal of Affective Disorders* vol.140: 300–305

216 *They leave hospital sooner* Ulrich, R. (1984) View through a window may influence recovery from surgery. *Science* vol.224: 420–421

216 *In the workplace* Won Sop Shin (2007) The influence of forest view through a window on job satisfaction and job stress. *Scandinavian Journal of Forest Research* vol.22: 248–253

216 *People who have had* Barton, J. & Pretty, J. (2010) What is the best dose of nature and green exercise for improving mental health? A multi-study analysis. *Environmental Science and Technology* vol.44: 3947–55

217 *There even appears to be* Sherwin, J., Reacher, M., Keogh, R., Khawaja, A., Mackey, D. & Foster, P. (2012) The association between time spent outdoors and myopia in children and adolescents: A systematic review and meta-analysis. *Ophthalmology* vol.119: 2141–51

217 *Research has found* Atchley, R., Strayer, D. & Atchley, P. (2012) Creativity in the wild: Improving creative reasoning through immersion in natural settings. *PLoS ONE* vol.7: e51474

217 *In other words* Miyazaki, Y., Lee, J., Park, B., Tsunetsugu, Y. & Matsunaga, K. (2011) Preventative medical effects of nature therapy. *Nihon Eiseigaku Zasshi, Japanese Journal of Hygiene* vol.66: 651–656

Acknowledgements

Firstly I would like to thank my amazing parents for all their love and support over the years. I have always been full of admiration for all you have done in your lives, and for who you are. I will always be grateful to have you as my parents.

Massive thanks to Mum especially for being the family editor! Thank goodness someone in the family isn't dyslexic. Thank you, Mum, for reading and editing all my academic work throughout the years and now a whole book. I really appreciate it.

Thank you to my wonderful son, Ivan. I cannot express how proud I am of you. You are such a special person; a true humanitarian, with a massive heart, a sharp intellect and a brilliant sense of humour. You bring light into the world.

Thanks to my brother Paul: you always have the ability to make me laugh, even through my tears at times! I am so grateful and treasure the relationship we have always had – I am very lucky to have a brother who is also my best friend.

Big thanks to the rest of my family, those who are here and those who are here in spirit. You all have a massive influence on me. I am inspired by you and I really appreciate knowing you are all around, in one way or the other.

Thank you to all my dear friends who have tragically died over the years. Thanks for all the fun times we had: "It is better to have loved and lost than never to have loved at all."

Thank you to Alex Barakan, my psychologist, mentor and friend. Thank you for so many things, but primarily for being the first person who made me believe in my intellectual capacity.

Thank you to Venerable Vajiragnana, my first Head Monk and my spiritual father. The gift of the Dhamma is immeasurable. And thanks to all the monks that I have been honoured to have known over the years: I am truly blessed to know you all and I will be forever grateful for your presence in my life.

Thank you to all at The London Buddhist Vihara. The Vihara is my spiritual home and I feel instantly happy when I walk in the door. Thank you for all you do for everyone who enters.

Thank you to my amazing agent Rosemary Scoular. I thought I would be lucky to get some advice from you, then you blew me away by being so kind and being willing to be my agent. Thank you for your consistent kindness, it is something I am deeply touched by. Also thank you for facilitating this book; it wouldn't have happened without you.

Thank you to dear Davina Rungasamy, I am so grateful to have you as my editing angel. You blessed my book with your wisdom and insight and gave me the confidence to believe it can help multiple people. You are such a rare and pure spirit.

Thank you to Stephanie Jackson for wanting to publish the book: I am so grateful for your enthusiasm and warmth from the moment I met you and throughout the process. It has meant everything to me.

Thank you to Stella Chili, the brilliant illustrator! I am so glad that I spent hours and hours trawling the internet to find you. The moment I saw your illustrations I knew you were the right person for this book. Your illlustrations are full of happiness and colour – they bring the book to life.

A big thank you to Yasia Williams and Alex Stetter from Aster, who have helped guide me through the whole process of illustrating and editing the book. It has been a total pleasure working with you both.

And finally thank you to all my clients over the years – thank you for the privilege of allowing me to help and guide you through the difficult times and the pleasure of seeing you into the good times!.

With my hand on my heart I bow with deep gratitude to you all for the love, joy, inspiration and happiness you bring into my life.